100 Task Cards
Text Evidence

Reproducible Mini-Passages With Key Questions to Boost Reading Comprehension Skills

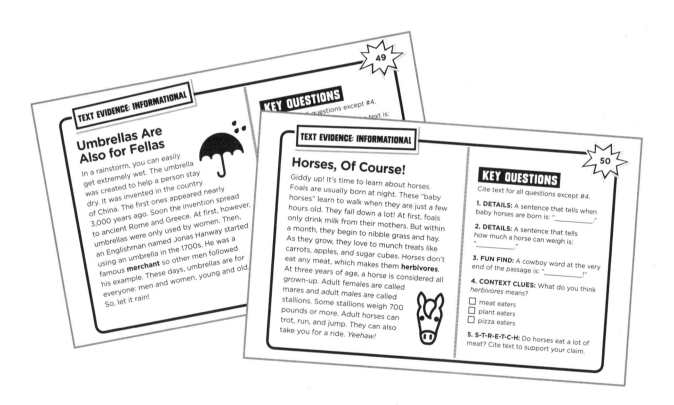

TEXT EVIDENCE: INFORMATIONAL

Umbrellas Are Also for Fellas

In a rainstorm, you can easily get extremely wet. The umbrella was created to help a person stay dry. It was invented in the country of China. The first ones appeared nearly 3,000 years ago. Soon the invention spread to ancient Rome and Greece. At first, however, umbrellas were only used by women. Then, an Englishman named Jonas Hanway started using an umbrella in the 1700s. He was a famous **merchant** so other men followed his example. These days, umbrellas are for everyone: men and women, young and old. So, let it rain!

TEXT EVIDENCE: INFORMATIONAL

49

KEY QUESTIONS

... questions except #4.

... text is:

50

Horses, Of Course!

Giddy up! It's time to learn about horses. Foals are usually born at night. These "baby horses" learn to walk when they are just a few hours old. They fall down a lot! At first, foals only drink milk from their mothers. But within a month, they begin to nibble grass and hay. As they grow, they love to munch treats like carrots, apples, and sugar cubes. Horses don't eat any meat, which makes them **herbivores**. At three years of age, a horse is considered all grown-up. Adult females are called mares and adult males are called stallions. Some stallions weigh 700 pounds or more. Adult horses can trot, run, and jump. They can also take you for a ride. *Yeehaw!*

KEY QUESTIONS

Cite text for all questions except #4.

1. DETAILS: A sentence that tells when baby horses are born is: "_____."

2. DETAILS: A sentence that tells how much a horse can weigh is: "_____."

3. FUN FIND: A cowboy word at the very end of the passage is: "_____!"

4. CONTEXT CLUES: What do you think *herbivores* means?
- ☐ meat eaters
- ☐ plant eaters
- ☐ pizza eaters

5. S-T-R-E-T-C-H: Do horses eat a lot of meat? Cite text to support your claim.

New York • Toronto • London • Auckland • Sydney
Mexico City • New Delhi • Hong Kong • Buenos Aires

Mini-passages written by Carol Ghiglieri and Justin Martin
Cover design by Tannaz Fassihi
Cover photo © Chris Windsor/Getty Images.
Interior design by Grafica, Inc.
Interior illustration by The Noun Project

ISBN: 978-1-338-11301-3

5 6 7 8 9 10   131   23 22 21 20 19

CONTENTS

INTRODUCTION

Welcome to *100 Task Cards: Text Evidence!*

Comprehension is more critical than ever. With the advent of rigorous state standards, students are now required to read a wide variety of complex texts—across the curriculum! Not only that, they're expected to locate specific information within those texts and cite it properly. Sound like a tall order? Indeed it is.

But don't despair. *100 Task Cards: Text Evidence* is here to help kids master this tricky skill in just minutes a day. Each card includes an informational or literary mini-passage along with key questions that give students plenty of practice in both locating and citing text evidence—the right way! The 100 high-interest task cards in this book also reinforce an understanding of:

- **Main Idea and Details**
- **Compare and Contrast**
- **Problem and Solution**
- **Cause and Effect**
- **Inference**
- **Fact and Opinion**
- **Character**
- **Setting**
- **Tone**
- **Theme**
- **Sequence of Events**
- **And more!**

The cards are designed for instant use—just photocopy, cut them apart, and they're good to go. The cards are also intended for flexible use. They're perfect for seatwork, centers, or meaningful homework. They're great for independent practice or work with partners, small groups, and even the whole class.

The questions on the cards will help students hone essential comprehension and text citation skills they'll rely on for a lifetime. And here's more good news: Because the mini-passages were written by professional authors with a gift for engaging young readers, kids will absolutely *love* them!

So what are you waiting for? Read on for tips that will help your students grow into confident, fluent, "deep" readers—quickly and painlessly. And don't forget to look for the other great books in this series, including *100 Task Cards: Literary Text* and *100 Task Cards: Informational Text*. The kids in your class will thank you.

TEACHING TIPS

About the 100 Text Evidence Task Cards

This book contains 50 informational text evidence cards and 50 literary text evidence cards. The mini-passages vary by topic, form, purpose, and tone in an effort to give students a wide variety of reading material—and meaningful practice—that correlates with current state standards. (For a list of the standards these cards address, see page 8.) Each card presents five questions, four of which hone text-evidence skills. Questions 1–3 provide prompts and writing frames that guide students to correctly cite text while question 5 challenges them to craft simple claims that incorporate text evidence. To prepare your students to succeed at citation, share the **First-Time Teaching Routine** on page 7 as well as the **Text Evidence Helper Sheet** on page 9.

The text evidence questions on the cards relate to must-know topics including main idea and details, compare and contrast, problem and solution, cause and effect, inference, fact and opinion, debate, sequence of events, character, setting, tone, theme, and more. We've also included a question related to context clues. This special feature is intended to boost your students' abilities to glean the meanings of unfamiliar words they encounter in all texts.

You will find the text type in the upper left-hand corner of each card. The mini-passages can be used in any order you choose. However, if you are teaching a certain topic or wish to help students hone a particular skill—such as understanding cause and effect—you can simply assign one or more cards from that category.

SAMPLE CARD: Here's a quick tour of a task card.

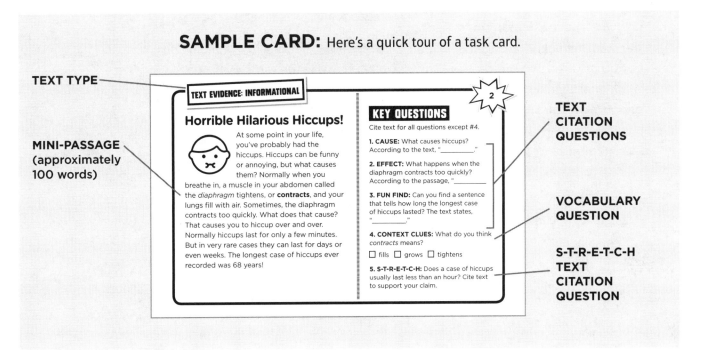

TEXT TYPE

MINI-PASSAGE (approximately 100 words)

TEXT CITATION QUESTIONS

VOCABULARY QUESTION

S-T-R-E-T-C-H TEXT CITATION QUESTION

About the Text Evidence Helper Sheet

This reproducible how-to page breaks down the seemingly tricky process of citing text into six easy steps. We encourage you to teach these steps explicitly as well as provide each student with a copy of the sheet. (See page 9.) It will come in handy as they tackle the questions on the task cards.

About the 12 Comprehension Helper Cards

To scaffold student learning, we've provided 12 Comprehension Helper Cards. (See pages 10–15.) These "bonus" cards, on topics ranging from main idea and details to tone and theme, are intended to provide age-perfect background information that will help students respond knowledgeably to the five questions on the task cards. We suggest you photocopy a set for each student to have at the ready.

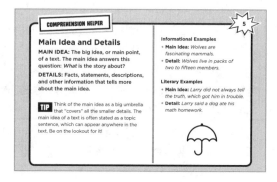

About the Answer Key

We've included a complete answer key. (See pages 67–80.) In the key, we've provided sample responses to the questions on all 100 cards. Please note that student answers will vary. Because many of the questions are open-ended and no two minds work exactly alike, we encourage you to accept— and applaud— all reasonable answers.

MAKING THE TASK CARDS

The task cards are easy to make. Just photocopy the pages and cut along the dashed lines.

- **Tip #1:** For sturdier cards, photocopy the pages on card stock and/or laminate them.

- **Tip #2:** To make the cards extra appealing, use different colors of paper or card stock for each category of card.

- **Tip #3:** To store the cards, use a plastic lunch bag or a recipe box. Or, hole punch the corner of each card and place on a key ring.

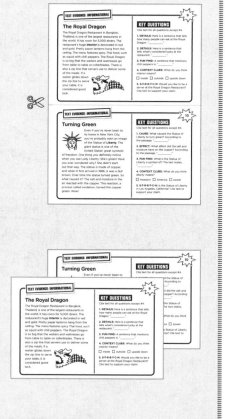

First-Time Teaching Routine

Any text will become accessible to students who bring strong reading strategies to the table. Here's an easy routine for introducing the task cards to your students for the very first time.

1. Display an enlarged version of the task card using an interactive whiteboard, document camera, or overhead projector.

2. Cover the mini-passage and display only the title. Read it aloud and invite students to predict what the text will be about.

3. Read the mini-passage aloud, slowly and clearly.

4. Boost fluency by inviting a student volunteer to read the mini-passage again using his or her best "performance" voice.

5. Discuss the mini-passage. Encourage students to comment and connect it to other articles and books they've read as well as to their own lives.

6. Call attention to the five key questions on the right of the mini-passage. Explain that all but question 4 will require students to cite text within the mini-passage.

7. Model how to properly "mine" the passage for complete sentences to cite as evidence. **TIP:** Use a highlighter to mark appropriate sentences in the passage.

8. Model the correct way to cite text by using a <u>writing stem</u> (such as *According to the text*), followed by a <u>comma or colon</u>, followed by the <u>exact text inside quotation marks</u>. NOTE: For the purpose of ease, all of the text-evidence questions should be answered with complete sentences. (For step-by-step how-to's on citing text, see the **Text Evidence Helper Sheet** on page 9.)

9. Number and record each answer on a chart pad.

10. Give your class a round of applause for successfully completing a task card. Now they're ready to tackle the cards independently.

INTEGRATING THE TASK CARDS INTO THE CLASSROOM

The task cards can be used in many ways. Here are ten quick ideas to maximize learning:

- Challenge students to complete one task card every morning.

- Invite partners to read the task cards together and respond in writing.

- Invite small groups to read, discuss, and respond to the task cards orally.

- Place the task cards in a learning center for students to enjoy independently.

- Carve out time to do a task card with the whole class a few times a week.

- Encourage individual students to build fluency by reading a task card aloud to the class. They can then solicit from fellow students answers to the questions.

- Laminate the task cards and place them in a recipe box for students to do after they've completed the rest of their work.

- Send the task cards home for students to complete with or without parental help.

- Provide students with designated notebooks for recording the answers to all of the task cards.

- Create a class chart, telling students to make a check mark each time they complete a task card. The first student to reach 100 wins a prize!

CONNECTION TO THE STANDARDS

The lessons in this book support the College and Career Readiness Anchor Standards for Reading for students in grades K–12. These broad standards, which serve as the basis of many state standards, were developed to establish rigorous educational expectations with the goal of providing students nationwide with a quality education that prepares them for college and careers. The chart below details how the lessons align with specific reading standards for literary and informational texts for students in grades 4 through 6.

These materials also address language standards, including skills in the conventions of standard English, knowledge of language, and vocabulary acquisition and use. In addition, students who write out their responses meet writing standards as they answer the questions about each mini-passage and demonstrate their ability to convey ideas about the text clearly and coherently.

INFORMATIONAL TEXT

Key Ideas and Details

- Refer to details and examples in a text when explaining what the text says explicitly and when drawing inferences from the text.

- Quote accurately from a text when explaining what the text says explicitly and when drawing inferences from the text.

- Cite textual evidence to support analysis of what the text says explicitly as well as inferences drawn from the text.

Craft and Structure

- Determine the meaning of general academic and domain-specific words or phrases in a text relevant to an age-appropriate topic.

- Describe the overall structure (e.g., chronology, comparison, cause/effect, problem/solution) of events, ideas, concepts, or information in a text or part of a text.

Integration of Knowledge and Ideas

- Explain how an author uses reasons and evidence to support particular points in a text.

- Analyze how a particular sentence, paragraph, chapter, or section fits into the overall structure of a text and contributes to the development of the ideas.

- Trace and evaluate the argument and specific claims in a text, distinguishing claims that are supported by reasons and evidence from claims that are not.

LITERARY TEXT

Key Ideas and Details

- Refer to details and examples in a text when explaining what the text says explicitly and when drawing inferences from the text.

- Determine a theme of a story, drama, or poem from details in the text; summarize the text.

- Describe in depth a character, setting, or event in a story or drama, drawing on specific details in the text (e.g., a character's thoughts, words, or actions).

- Quote accurately from a text when explaining what the text says explicitly and when drawing inferences from the text.

- Cite textual evidence to support analysis of what the text says explicitly as well as inferences drawn from the text.

- Describe how a particular story or drama unfolds in a series of episodes as well as how the characters respond or change as the plot moves toward a resolution.

Craft and Structure

- Determine the meaning of words and phrases as they are used in a text, including those that allude to significant characters found in mythology (e.g., Herculean).

- Compare and contrast two or more characters, settings, or events in a story or drama, drawing on specific details in the text (e.g., how characters interact).

TEXT EVIDENCE HELPER SHEET

SAMPLE CARD

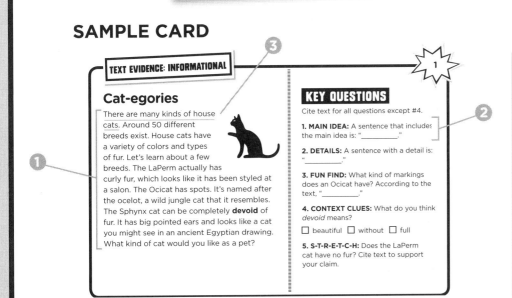

TEXT EVIDENCE: INFORMATIONAL

Cat-egories

There are many kinds of house cats. Around 50 different breeds exist. House cats have a variety of colors and types of fur. Let's learn about a few breeds. The LaPerm actually has curly fur, which looks like it has been styled at a salon. The Ocicat has spots. It's named after the ocelot, a wild jungle cat that it resembles. The Sphynx cat can be completely **devoid** of fur. It has big pointed ears and looks like a cat you might see in an ancient Egyptian drawing. What kind of cat would you like as a pet?

KEY QUESTIONS

Cite text for all questions except #4.

1. MAIN IDEA: A sentence that includes the main idea is: "_____."

2. DETAILS: A sentence with a detail is: "_____."

3. FUN FIND: What kind of markings does an Ocicat have? According to the text, "_____."

4. CONTEXT CLUES: What do you think *devoid* means?

☐ beautiful ☐ without ☐ full

5. S-T-R-E-T-C-H: Does the LaPerm cat have no fur? Cite text to support your claim.

SENTENCE STEMS

* According to the text,
* The article states:
* The story says,
* The passage reveals:
* The author feels,
* The writer believes,
* The sentence says,
* The sentence states:
* One example is,

How to cite text in 6 easy steps!

1. Carefully read the mini-passage once or more.

2. Carefully read the first text citation question.

3. Go back to the passage and locate a sentence that answers the question.
   TIP: If possible, underline the sentence in pen.

4. Copy a suggested sentence stem or create your own.
   (See options above, at right.)
   TIP: A stem always starts with a capital letter and ends with a comma or colon.
   (Commas and colons can be used interchangeably.)

   EXAMPLE *A sentence that includes the main idea is:*

5. Follow the sentence stem with quotation marks that contain the exact and entire sentence pulled from the mini-passage.
   TIP: The sentence should begin with a capital letter and end with a punctuation mark.

   EXAMPLE *A sentence that includes the main idea is:*
   "There are many kinds of house cats."

6. Proofread your work.

Congratulations, you just learned how to cite text evidence!

Informational Text

Text that provides facts and information to readers. Synonym: Nonfiction.

TIP *Before reading*, think about what you already know about the topic. Also think about questions you'd like answered in the text. *During reading*, take your time. Try to determine the main idea and key details. Reread any confusing parts. *After reading*, reflect on what you just read. Talk about the text with a classmate.

Examples

- *news stories*
- *textbooks*
- *business memos*
- *magazine articles*
- *advertisements*
- *personal essays*
- *humor essays*
- *nonfiction books*
- *health care pamphlets*
- *assembly instructions*
- *campaign information*
- *biographies*
- *sports articles*
- *history titles*
- *editorials*
- *recipes*
- *opinion pieces*
- *memoirs*

Literary Text

A piece of writing, such as a story or poem, that has the purpose of telling a tale or entertaining.

TIP *Before reading*, look at the title. What do you think the story will be about? *During reading*, stop and make predictions about what will happen next. Reread the parts you especially like or find confusing. *After reading*, reflect on the story. Compare it to other books and movies, as well as your own life. Ask yourself, "What did the author want to tell me? What did I learn?"

Examples

- *fantasy*
- *science fiction*
- *thrillers*
- *legends*
- *folktales*
- *tall tales*
- *horror*
- *romance*
- *tragedy*
- *adventure stories*
- *friendship stories*
- *realistic fiction*
- *mysteries*
- *comedies*
- *fairy tales*
- *fables*
- *drama*
- *poems*
- *short stories*
- *plays*

COMPREHENSION HELPER

Text Evidence

Exact words, phrases, or sentences in a text that provide information, answer a question, or support a claim.

TIP When citing text, frame your text evidence with a sentence stem such as, *According to the text*. Follow that with a comma or colon (, or :). Then place the exact words from the text inside the quotation marks. (See examples on the right.)

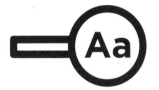

Informational Examples

- *According to the text, "Grizzly bears usually emerge from hibernation in early spring."*

- *The author states: "Medieval castles ranged from simple wood structures to massive stone compounds."*

Literary Examples

- *The story says, "Lydia's bedroom was neat and orderly, much like her brain."*

- *An example of a simile in the story is: "Today, Jamal felt as free as a bird."*

COMPREHENSION HELPER

Context Clues

Hints readers use to figure out the meaning of an unknown word in a text. Context clues can come before or after the unknown word.

TIP Authors use many words you may not know. But nearby words, phrases, and sentences can offer important clues to the unfamiliar word's definition. As you read, play detective and search for clues to the mystery word's meaning. This will help you improve your understanding and your vocabulary without reaching for a dictionary.

Examples

- **Definition Clues:** *The unknown word is defined in the text.*

- **Example Clues:** *An example of the unknown word is provided in the text.*

- **Synonym Clues:** *A word with a similar meaning is near the unknown word.*

- **Antonym Clues:** *A word with the opposite meaning is near the unknown word.*

Main Idea and Details

MAIN IDEA: The big idea, or main point, of a text. The main idea answers this question: *What* is the text about?

DETAILS: Facts, statements, descriptions, and other information that tells more about the main idea.

TIP Think of the main idea as a big umbrella that "covers" all the smaller details. The main idea of a text is often stated as a topic sentence, which can appear anywhere in the text. Be on the lookout for it!

Informational Examples

- **Main Idea:** *Wolves are fascinating mammals.*
- **Detail:** *Wolves live in packs of three to fifteen members.*

Literary Examples

- **Main Idea:** *Larry did not always tell the truth, which got him in trouble.*
- **Detail:** *Larry said a dog ate his math homework.*

COMPREHENSION HELPER

6

Compare and Contrast

COMPARE: To look closely at two or more things (people, animals, places, objects, concepts, etc.) to see how they are similar.

CONTRAST: To look closely at two or more things to see how they are different.

TIP To compare and contrast elements of a text, be on the lookout for signal words. *Both, in common, and, too*, and *also* relate to similarities. *Differ, however, only, while*, and *on the other hand* relate to differences.

Informational Examples

- **Compare:** *Squirrels and mice are rodents. They both have claws.*
- **Contrast:** *Squirrels have big, bushy tails while mice have long, thin tails.*

Literary Examples

- **Compare:** *Min and Megan were both tall, athletic girls who played basketball.*
- **Contrast:** *Min was funny and always calm. On the other hand, Megan was sensitive and often nervous.*

COMPREHENSION HELPER

Problem and Solution

PROBLEM: A difficulty that needs fixing.

SOLUTION: How that difficulty gets repaired or resolved.

TIP Some texts present a challenging situation to engage readers, then offer one or more solutions to the problem. Words that signal a problem include *question, problem, dilemma, issue, puzzle, need*, and *trouble*. Words that signal a solution include *answer, result, solve, improve, prevent, invent, fix, correct*, and *remedy*. In literary texts this is often referred to as "Conflict and Resolution."

Informational Examples

- **Problem:** *The fact that kids were getting polio was a big dilemma.*
- **Solution:** *A doctor solved the problem by developing a vaccine.*

Literary Examples

- **Problem:** *Terrance did not have enough money to buy a new bike.*
- **Solution:** *What was Terrance's answer? He opened a lemonade stand!*

COMPREHENSION HELPER

Cause and Effect

CAUSE: The action or reason something happens.

EFFECT: The result or outcome of that action.

TIP Some texts show a relationship between something that happens and its outcome. Words that signal cause and effect include *due to, as a result, since, therefore, because of, so, for this reason, so that, in order to*, and *led to*.

Informational Examples

- **Cause:** *Lightning strikes an old house.*
- **Effect:** *Due to the lightning, the house catches on fire.*

Literary Examples

- **Cause:** *Jana accidentally leaves the back door wide open.*
- **Effect:** *As a result, a curious raccoon wanders into her kitchen.*

COMPREHENSION HELPER

Inference

Drawing a conclusion about a text based on clues within it.

TIP Text clues are words or details that help you figure out an unstated idea. To make an inference, combine clues in the text with your own background knowledge to figure out what the author is *really* trying to tell you.

Informational Examples

- *If a nonfiction book says, "Harriet Tubman walked though the dangerous, dark woods all by herself," you could <u>infer</u> that she was very brave.*
- *If an article states, "Sugar tastes sweet, but can have sour consequences," you could <u>infer</u> that eating too much sugar is bad for your health.*

Literary Examples

- *If a fiction book says, "Carlos had very sweaty palms," you could <u>infer</u> that he was nervous.*
- *If a fiction story states, "Ashley got chills and began to cough," you could <u>infer</u> that she was getting sick.*

COMPREHENSION HELPER

Fact and Opinion

FACT: A piece of information that is true. Facts don't vary.

OPINION: A personal belief or feeling. Opinions do vary.

TIP Some texts include facts, opinion, or both. Words that signal facts include *proof, know, data, indicate, discovered,* and *research shows.* Words that signal opinions include *believe, think, wish, expect, disagree, probably, hope, seem to, viewpoint,* and *feel.*

Examples

- **Fact:** *I know dolphins are mammals.*
- **Opinion:** *I think dolphins are cute.*
- **Fact:** *My book states that George Washington was the first U.S. president.*
- **Opinion:** *The author believes George Washington was the very best president.*
- **Fact:** *Research shows that smoking can cause cancer.*
- **Opinion:** *My parents feel smoking is an awful habit.*
- **Fact:** *Scientists have discovered more than two million different insects.*
- **Opinion:** *I don't care for bugs!*

Character and Setting

CHARACTER: One of the individuals in a story.

SETTING: The place and time in which a story happens.

TIP To better understand <u>characters</u>, read for details that describe them. What makes them unique? To better understand a <u>setting</u>, read for details that tell where and when the story is happening.

Character Examples

- *Harry Potter*
- *The Big Bad Wolf*
- *Mary Poppins*
- *Willy Wonka*
- *Katniss Everdeen*
- *The Little Engine That Could*
- *Goldilocks*
- *Percy Jackson*
- *Greg Heffley*
- *Icarus*

Setting Examples

- *haunted house*
- *New York City*
- *school*
- *tree house*
- *zoo*
- *ancient Greece*
- *Mars*
- *magic forest*
- *under the sea*
- *kid's bedroom*
- *log cabin*

Tone and Theme

TONE: The way the narrator feels about the events, settings, and characters in a story.

THEME: The big idea or message of a story.

TIP To figure out the <u>tone</u> of the story, ask: *How did the narrator feel about the people, setting, and events in the story?* To figure out the <u>theme</u> of a story, ask: *How did it end? What was the author trying to tell me? How did the characters change? What did I learn?*

Tone Examples

- *gloomy*
- *fantastical*
- *bossy*
- *annoyed*
- *stuck-up*
- *dorky*
- *zany*
- *enthusiastic*
- *cynical*
- *scared*
- *jealous*
- *lonely*

Theme Examples

- *Be true to your own values.*
- *Family loyalty is very important.*
- *Appearances can be deceiving.*
- *Differences make people special.*
- *Courage comes from facing fears.*

100 TEXT EVIDENCE TASK CARDS

1

Cat-egories

There are many kinds of house cats. Around 50 different breeds exist. House cats have a variety of colors and types of fur. Let's learn about a few breeds. The LaPerm actually has curly fur, which looks like it has been styled at a salon. The Ocicat has spots. It's named after the ocelot, a wild jungle cat that it resembles. The Sphynx cat can be completely **devoid** of fur. It has big pointed ears and looks like a cat you might see in an ancient Egyptian drawing. What kind of cat would you like as a pet?

KEY QUESTIONS

Cite text for all questions except #4.

1. MAIN IDEA: A sentence that includes the main idea is: "_____."

2. DETAILS: A sentence with a detail is: "_____."

3. FUN FIND: What kind of markings does an Ocicat have? According to the text, "_____."

4. CONTEXT CLUES: What do you think *devoid* means?

☐ beautiful ☐ without ☐ full

5. S-T-R-E-T-C-H: Does the LaPerm cat have no fur? Cite text to support your claim.

2

Horrible Hilarious Hiccups!

At some point in your life, you've probably had the hiccups. Hiccups can be funny or annoying, but what causes them? Normally when you breathe in, a muscle in your abdomen called the *diaphragm* tightens, or **contracts**, and your lungs fill with air. Sometimes, the diaphragm contracts too quickly. What does that cause? That causes you to hiccup over and over. Normally hiccups last for only a few minutes. But in very rare cases they can last for days or even weeks. The longest case of hiccups ever recorded was 68 years!

KEY QUESTIONS

Cite text for all questions except #4.

1. CAUSE: What causes hiccups? According to the text, "_____."

2. EFFECT: What happens when the diaphragm contracts too quickly? According to the passage, "_____."

3. FUN FIND: Can you find a sentence that tells how long the longest case of hiccups lasted? The text states, "_____."

4. CONTEXT CLUES: What do you think *contracts* means?

☐ fills ☐ grows ☐ tightens

5. S-T-R-E-T-C-H: Does a case of hiccups usually last less than an hour? Cite text to support your claim.

Snow and Salt

Snow and salt have a surprising amount of things in common. Both are white and both consist of crystals. Looking at a snowflake under a microscope, you can see little ice crystals in the shape of a star. If you study an **individual** salt crystal, you'll see it's shaped like a tiny cube. You can put both snow and salt in your mouth. They sure don't taste the same though. In your mouth, snow melts into plain water, while salt tastes, well, salty. Here's another difference. You can build a snowman, but you can't build a saltman.

KEY QUESTIONS

Cite text for all questions except #4.

1. COMPARE: This sentence shows a similarity between snow and salt: "_____."

2. CONTRAST: This sentence shows a difference between snow and salt: "_____."

3. FUN FIND: This sentence describes the shape of a salt crystal: "_____."

4. CONTEXT CLUES: What do you think *individual* means?

☐ sour ☐ single ☐ salty

5. S-T-R-E-T-C-H: Is a snowflake shaped like a tiny cube? Cite text to support your claim.

The Stinkiest Animals on Earth!

You've heard of *gorillas*, but have you ever heard of zorillas? Zorillas are also known as striped polecats. They are related to skunks. They're about two feet long and they're covered with black fur and white stripes. They have flat faces, small ears, and long bushy tails. Their paws have claws, which they use to dig up food. Zorillas generally live alone or in small family groups. They communicate with growls and high-pitched screams. They also communicate with scent. Like skunks, zorillas spray a **foul-smelling** scent to keep predators away. In fact, zorillas are considered the stinkiest animals on Earth!

KEY QUESTIONS

Cite text for all questions except #4.

1. DESCRIPTION: A sentence that describes how zorillas look is: "_____."

2. DESCRIPTION: A sentence that describes how zorillas communicate is: "_____."

3. FUN FIND: Can you find a sentence that gives another name for zorillas? The author states: "_____."

4. CONTEXT CLUES: What do you think *foul-smelling* means?

☐ nice-smelling ☐ bad-smelling
☐ sweet-smelling

5. S-T-R-E-T-C-H: Would you like to have a zorilla for a pet? Cite text to support your claim.

Should Kids Have Chores?

Do you have to do chores at home? When it comes to this issue, different people have very different ideas. Some people think that having chores is important for kids. They say chores help kids develop responsibility and **self-reliance**. They also say that having chores will encourage kids to care about the needs of others. But those against having kids do chores think it is a waste of their time. They argue that kids should be focused on their homework and other activities that will bring them success. They say that kids have enough to do without worrying about household tasks. What do you say?

KEY QUESTIONS

Cite text for all questions except #4.

1. PRO: This sentence argues in favor of chores for kids: "_____."

2. CON: This sentence argues against chores for kids: "_____."

3. FUN FIND: Do people agree on this topic? According to the text, "_____."

4. CONTEXT CLUES: What do you think *self-reliance* means?

☐ selfishness ☐ stress
☐ independence

5. S-T-R-E-T-C-H: Should children do chores around the house? Cite text to support your claim.

Dandy Dandelions

The dandelion is a very common plant with yellow flowers. Many people consider these weeds a **nuisance** and try to remove them from their yards. Such people are just wrong about dandelions. Dandelions are beautiful. They're also edible. Dandelions are eaten in salads. They are even used to make homemade root beer. Most of all, I think dandelions are fun. Late in the summer, their yellow flowers are replaced by seeds. If you blow on them, the seeds float through the air like tiny parachutes. Dandelions are just dandy with me.

KEY QUESTIONS

Cite text for all questions except #4.

1. FACT: A fact in the text is: "_____."

2. OPINION: An opinion in the text is: "_____."

3. FUN FIND: A sentence that compares seeds to something else is: "_____."

4. CONTEXT CLUES: What do you think *nuisance* means?

☐ a plant ☐ a joy ☐ a bother

5. S-T-R-E-T-C-H: Are dandelions a good or bad plant? Cite text to support your claim.

Pompeii

A famous volcano erupted nearly two thousand years ago. The date was August 24 in the year 79 AD. The name of that volcano was Mount Vesuvius.  The volcano's powerful eruption buried a whole city called Pompeii. Many lives were lost. Over the years, people forgot about the buried city. Then, in the 1700s, archaeologists discovered the lost city of Pompeii. Here's the amazing thing: Beneath the ash, they found a community frozen in time. Many buildings and houses were perfectly **preserved**. With the discovery of Pompeii, modern people were able to learn a great deal about life in ancient times.

KEY QUESTIONS

Cite text for all questions except #4.

1. SEQUENCE: The first thing that happens in the text is: "_____."

2. SEQUENCE: Something that happens later in the text is: "_____."

3. FUN FIND: I thought this detail was interesting: "_____"

4. CONTEXT CLUES: What do you think *preserved* means?

☐ kept as original   ☐ very old
☐ totally destroyed

5. S-T-R-E-T-C-H: Did archaeologists discover Pompeii before or after the year 1600? Cite text to support your claim.

All About Deserts

A desert is a very common **habitat**. About one third of the Earth is covered in desert. A desert is an area that usually gets less than 10 inches of rain in a year. Some well-known deserts include the Gobi Desert in Asia and the Sahara Desert in Africa. Even though deserts are dry, they are home to many plants and animals. Desert creatures include lizards, foxes, and  penguins. Hold on! Penguins? Yes, even though deserts are dry, they don't have to be hot places. Antarctica is a cold, dry place. So Antarctica is one of the world's many deserts.

KEY QUESTIONS

Cite text for all questions except #4.

1. MAIN IDEA: A sentence that includes the main idea is, "_____."

2. DETAILS: A sentence with a detail is, "_____."

3. FUN FIND: A sentence that mentions three desert animals is: "_____."

4. CONTEXT CLUES: What do you think *habitat* means?

☐ a small habit   ☐ clothing
☐ an animal home

5. S-T-R-E-T-C-H: Would you like to live in a desert? Cite text to support your claim.

TEXT EVIDENCE: INFORMATIONAL

The Royal Dragon

The Royal Dragon Restaurant in Bangkok, Thailand, is one of the largest restaurants in the world. It has room for 5,000 diners. The restaurant's huge **interior** is decorated in red and gold. Pretty paper lanterns hang from the ceiling. The menu features spicy Thai food, such as squid with chili peppers. The Royal Dragon is so big that the waiters and waitresses go from table to table on rollerblades. There is also a zip line that servers use to deliver some of the meals. If a waiter glides down the zip line to serve your table, it is considered good luck.

KEY QUESTIONS

Cite text for all questions except #4.

1. DETAILS: Here is a sentence that tells how many people can eat at the Royal Dragon: "_____."

2. DETAILS: Here is a sentence that tells what's considered lucky at the restaurant: "_____."

3. FUN FIND: A sentence that mentions chili peppers is: "_____."

4. CONTEXT CLUES: What do you think *interior* means?

☐ inside ☐ outside ☐ upside down

5. S-T-R-E-T-C-H: Would you like to be a server at the Royal Dragon Restaurant? Cite text to support your claim.

TEXT EVIDENCE: INFORMATIONAL

Turning Green

Even if you've never been to its home in New York City, you've probably seen an image of the Statue of **Liberty**. The giant statue is one of the United States' great symbols of freedom. One thing you definitely notice when you see Lady Liberty: She's green! Have you ever wondered why? She didn't start out that way. The statue is made of copper, and when it first arrived in 1886, it was a dull brown. Over time the statue turned green. So what caused it? The salt and moisture in the air reacted with the copper. This reaction, a process called oxidation, turned the copper green. Wow!

KEY QUESTIONS

Cite text for all questions except #4.

1. CAUSE: What caused the Statue of Liberty to turn green? According to the passage, "_____."

2. EFFECT: What effect did the salt and moisture have on the copper? According to the passage, "_____."

3. FUN FIND: What is the Statue of Liberty a symbol of? The text states, "_____."

4. CONTEXT CLUES: What do you think *liberty* means?

☐ freedom ☐ America ☐ power

5. S-T-R-E-T-C-H: Is the Statue of Liberty in Los Angeles, California? Cite text to support your claim.

Reflexes

Something threatens to harm you. Your reflexes kick in. Have you ever had a doctor tap your knee and out swings your leg? This is a reflex. The reason we have reflexes is for quick protection, without even having to think. Humans have many different reflexes. For example, an object flying toward your eye will make you blink. If you touch something hot, your hand will draw back **involuntarily**. Even sneezing is a reflex. You can't just decide to sneeze and make yourself do it. If something irritates your nose, you will sneeze to get rid of it. Hooray for reflexes! They keep us safe.

KEY QUESTIONS

Cite text for all questions except #4.

1. CAUSE: A sentence that states the cause is: "_____."

2. EFFECT: A sentence that states the effect is: "_____."

3. FUN FIND: This sentence tells what happens if something bothers your nose: "_____."

4. CONTEXT CLUES: What do you think *involuntarily* means?

☐ quickly ☐ not a volunteer
☐ without thinking

5. S-T-R-E-T-C-H: Are reflexes helpful or harmful? Cite text to support your claim.

Bugs for Breakfast?

In many parts of the world, people eat insects. In fact, about 80 percent of the world's population regularly eats bugs. That sounds pretty gross! There are several reasons people eat insects. For one thing, insects are **plentiful**. Bugs are all around us, and they provide a good source of protein. Eating bugs is also cheap, and some countries don't have enough money or land to raise farm animals. And then there's taste. People who eat bugs say they're delicious. That's hard to believe. Grasshoppers, they say, taste salty and spicy. Termites taste like carrots. And tarantulas taste nutty. Sound yummy?

KEY QUESTIONS

Cite text for all questions except #4.

1. FACT: A fact in the text is: "_____."

2. OPINION: An opinion in the text is: "_____."

3. FUN FIND: I thought this fact was interesting: "_____."

4. CONTEXT CLUES: What do you think *plentiful* means?

☐ delicious ☐ in large number
☐ easy to catch

5. S-T-R-E-T-C-H: Are you in favor of people eating bugs? Cite text to support your claim.

Big Planet, Small Planet

Let's learn about Mercury and Neptune! They have some things in common. They are both planets. They both travel around the sun. All the planets that **orbit** the sun, including Earth, make up what's called the solar system. But Mercury and Neptune are different, too. Mercury is the smallest planet in the solar system, while Neptune is quite large. Here's another difference. Mercury is the warmest planet in the solar system, while Neptune is very cold. During a day on Mercury, the temperature can reach 800 degrees. Neptune is furthest from the sun. Its temperature can drop to more than 350 degrees below zero. *Brrrrrr!*

KEY QUESTIONS

Cite text for all questions except #4.

1. COMPARE: In the text, a similarity between Mercury and Neptune is: "_____."

2. CONTRAST: In the text, a difference between the two planets is: "_____."

3. FUN FIND: This sentence tells how cold Neptune can get: "_____."

4. CONTEXT CLUES: What do you think *orbit* means?

☐ travel fast ☐ travel in a straight line
☐ travel around

5. S-T-R-E-T-C-H: Can humans live on the planet of Mercury? Cite text to support your claim.

Every Four Years

Every four years we elect a president of the United States. Here's how the process unfolds. First, about eighteen months before election day, Democratic and Republican candidates announce their plans to run for president. In the following months, they give speeches and hold debates. They try to win supporters. Then, beginning in February of the election year, states across the country hold their primaries. Primaries are elections to choose one Democratic and one Republican candidate. They're a bit like the playoffs in sports. Once these candidates are chosen, they **campaign** until November. Finally, in November, Americans vote to decide who will be the next president.

KEY QUESTIONS

Cite text for all questions except #4.

1. SEQUENCE: According to the text, the thing that starts the process is: "_____."

2. SEQUENCE: According to the text, the last thing that happens is: "_____."

3. FUN FIND: What are the primaries "a bit like"? The author says, "_____."

4. CONTEXT CLUES: What do you think *campaign* means?

☐ try to get people to vote for you
☐ try to meet leaders
☐ try to help animals

5. S-T-R-E-T-C-H: Are new presidents elected in October? Cite text to support your claim.

The Mighty Blue Whale

The blue whale is the largest creature on Earth. These ocean mammals are truly massive. Adults can grow to 100 feet long and weigh more than 200 tons. The tongue of a blue whale can weigh as much as an entire elephant, and its heart can weigh as much as a car! Blue whales eat krill, which are tiny ocean creatures. They can consume four tons of krill in a single day! To match their huge size, blue whales are very loud. To communicate they **emit** moans and clicks. Other blue whales can hear them from up to 1,000 miles away. These creatures deserve the name "king of the ocean."

KEY QUESTIONS

Cite text for all questions except #4.

1. MAIN IDEA: A sentence that includes the main idea is: "_____."

2. DETAILS: A sentence with an important detail is: "_____."

3. FUN FIND: How much krill can whales eat in one day? According to the text, "_____."

4. CONTEXT CLUES: What do you think *emit* means?

☐ hear   ☐ believe   ☐ send out

5. S-T-R-E-T-C-H: Why do blue whales deserve the name "king of the ocean"? Cite text to support your claim.

Elisha Otis's Great Invention

In the old days, most buildings were small. Tall buildings were troublesome because people would get exhausted walking up and down all the steps. What was the solution? Elisha Otis invented the modern elevator. Simple elevators had been around for hundreds of years. But Otis's 1853 invention had a **crucial** new feature. It had a safety break so that the elevator couldn't fall. Otis's first elevators ran on steam power. After a few years, electric elevators were introduced. Elevators made it possible to build really tall buildings. Aren't you glad skyscrapers have elevators?

KEY QUESTIONS

Cite text for all questions except #4.

1. PROBLEM: The problem in the text is: "_____."

2. SOLUTION: The solution in the text is: "_____."

3. FUN FIND: I thought this fact was extra interesting: "_____."

4. CONTEXT CLUES: What do you think *crucial* means?

☐ funny   ☐ intelligent
☐ very important

5. S-T-R-E-T-C-H: Why is *Elisha Otis's Great Invention* a good title for this passage? Cite text to support your claim.

The Voyage of the *Titanic*

The word *titanic* means "huge." Thus it was the perfect name for the massive steamship completed in 1912. The *Titanic* was the biggest steamship of its time. It stretched as long as three football fields and stood as tall as a 17-story building. It was constructed of steel. The *Titanic* could carry 3,500 people. Its builders made use of the most advanced shipbuilding techniques of the time. For this reason, folks said the ship was "unsinkable." Tragically, it collided with an iceberg on its very first voyage and sank. Many of those on board **perished**.

KEY QUESTIONS

Cite text for all questions except #4.

1. DESCRIPTION: How big was the *Titanic*? The author states, " _____."

2. DESCRIPTION: What was the ship made of? According to the text, "_____."

3. FUN FIND: How many people could the *Titanic* carry? The text states, "_____."

4. CONTEXT CLUES: What do you think *perished* means?

☐ rounded ☐ died ☐ soft

5. S-T-R-E-T-C-H: Why did people think the *Titanic* was unsinkable? Cite text to support your claim.

Is It a Meteor or a Meteorite?

It's easy to confuse the words *meteor* and *meteorite*. So what are they, and what's the difference between them? Meteors and meteorites are related. Both are small bodies from outer space that enter Earth's atmosphere. A meteor is an object that burns up as it travels through our solar system. Meteors leave a visible trail behind them. They are sometimes called "shooting stars," even though they're not really stars. Unlike meteors, meteorites don't completely burn up. Instead, they fall to Earth. Between five and ten meteorites **strike** Earth each year.

KEY QUESTIONS

Cite text for all questions except #4.

1. COMPARE: How are meteors and meteorites similar? According to the text, "_____."

2. CONTRAST: Name one way meteors are different from meteorites. According to the text, "_____."

3. FUN FIND: How many meteorites hit Earth each year? The author states, "_____."

4. CONTEXT CLUES: What do you think *strike* means?

☐ hit ☐ burn ☐ circle

5. S-T-R-E-T-C-H: Why do you think meteors are called "shooting stars"? Cite text to support your claim.

An Amazing Landing on the Hudson River

Most airplanes take off and land without a problem. But on January 15, 2009, things didn't go as planned. A few minutes after US Airways Flight 1549 took off from New York City, the jet crossed paths with a flock of geese. Some of the birds got trapped in the plane's engines, and the jet suddenly lost all power. The pilot, Chesley Sullenberger, knew that the plane would soon crash. What did he do? Sullenberger stayed calm. He **navigated** the jet over to the Hudson River so he could land the plane on water. It was a risky move, but he managed to get the plane down safely. All 155 people on board were safe.

KEY QUESTIONS

Cite text for all questions except #4.

1. PROBLEM: What problem is described in this passage? According to the text, "_____."

2. SOLUTION: How does Sullenberger solve it? The author states, "_____."

3. FUN FIND: Did Sullenberger panic when he realized the plane would soon crash? According to the text, "_____."

4. CONTEXT CLUES: What do you think *navigated* means?

☐ hurried   ☐ landed   ☐ steered

5. S-T-R-E-T-C-H: Do you think Sullenberger is a hero? Cite text to support your claim.

How Plants Make Food

Plants have an amazing way of making food. The first step is very familiar. A plant drinks water. It drinks by using its roots to draw water up from the ground. Then comes the second step. A plant's leaves **absorb** sunlight. Next, the plant mixes together water, sunlight, and a gas called carbon dioxide. This makes sugar, which is the plant's food. The plant uses the sugar to grow. While making sugar, the plant also makes something it doesn't need: oxygen. What happens then? The plant sends the oxygen out into the air. Guess who needs oxygen? People and animals do. Thanks, plants!

KEY QUESTIONS

Cite text for all questions except #4.

1. SEQUENCE: The first step is, "_____."

2. SEQUENCE: The second step is, "_____."

3. FUN FIND: A sentence that tells who needs oxygen is, "_____."

4. CONTEXT CLUES: What do you think *absorb* means?

☐ get rid of   ☐ soak up   ☐ totally adorable

5. S-T-R-E-T-C-H: What three things do plants mix together to make their food? Cite text to support your claim.

TEXT EVIDENCE: INFORMATIONAL

The Best Pizza?

Most people agree that pizza is delicious. But when it comes to deciding *which* pizza is best, opinions **diverge** and tempers can get heated! The two major styles of pizza are Chicago-style and New York-style. Both are round pies, with a bready crust. Both feature tomato sauce, cheese, and other toppings. But while New York-style pizza has a thin crust, the crust on Chicago-style pizza is thick. New York pizzas are flat, and you can eat them with your hands, but Chicago pizzas are deep-dish and you need a fork and knife. Some people would rather not choose between the two styles. They love both!

KEY QUESTIONS

Cite text for all questions except #4.

1. COMPARE: A sentence that tells how the two pizzas are similar is: "_____."

2. CONTRAST: A sentence that tells how the two pizzas are different is: "_____."

3. FUN FIND: What is something that most people agree on? According to the text: "_____."

4. CONTEXT CLUES: What do you think *diverge* means?

☐ spill ☐ agree ☐ divide

5. S-T-R-E-T-C-H: Which pizza sounds better to you—Chicago-style or New York-style? Cite text to support your claim.

TEXT EVIDENCE: INFORMATIONAL

Wide World of Rodents

Rodents are a type of mammal. They have **atypical** teeth that keep growing throughout their lives. They gnaw on things to file back their teeth. I think they look silly when they gnaw. Rats, mice, and squirrels aren't the only rodents. There are about 1,500 different kinds, including chipmunks, gerbils, beavers, and porcupines. The biggest rodent is the capybara. Capybaras live in South America and can weigh around 100 pounds. Now, that's one scary rodent!

KEY QUESTIONS

Cite text for all questions except #4.

1. FACT: A fact in the text is: "_____."

2. OPINION: An opinion in the text is: "_____."

3. FUN FIND: Another interesting fact in the text is: "_____."

4. CONTEXT CLUES: What do you think *atypical* means?

☐ usual ☐ unusual ☐ very small

5. S-T-R-E-T-C-H: Is a beaver the largest type of rodent? Cite text to support your claim.

Life on Other Planets?

Is there life elsewhere in the universe? Some scientists would say yes. Because the universe is so vast, chances are good that somewhere out there life exists. Other planets circling other stars could be suitable homes to living creatures. Those creatures might not even look anything like living creatures on Earth. But some scientists would say no. They'd argue that the Earth is the only place right for life. Every other place might have problems like being too hot, too cold, or too dry. Other planets might not have breathable air. Maybe the Earth is **unique** in all the universe. What do you think?

KEY QUESTIONS

Cite text for all questions except #4.

1. PRO: This sentence argues that life might exist elsewhere in the universe: "_____."

2. CON: This sentence argues that life is only on Earth: "_____."

3. FUN FIND: This sentence states the debate topic: "_____."

4. CONTEXT CLUES: What do you think *unique* means?

☐ one of many ☐ one of a kind
☐ bubbly

5. S-T-R-E-T-C-H: Do you think life exists on other planets? Cite text to support your claim.

The Famous Leaning Tower

Have you ever heard of the Leaning Tower of Pisa? That's *Pisa*, not *pizza*! The Tower of Pisa is a very old tower in the city of Pisa, in Italy. It's an extremely popular **tourist attraction** for an unusual reason. The tower is tilting. Most buildings, of course, stand up straight, but the

Tower of Pisa has been leaning for hundreds of years. What is causing the tower to tilt? It was built on soil that was too soft to support it. Over the years, engineers have developed ways to keep it from toppling over. So far, at least!

KEY QUESTIONS

Cite text for all questions except #4.

1. CAUSE: What is causing the tower to lean? The text states, "_____."

2. EFFECT: What is the effect of building the tower on soft soil? According to the text, "_____."

3. FUN FIND: Can you find a sentence that tells where the Tower of Pisa is located? The text says, "_____."

4. CONTEXT CLUES: What do you think *tourist attraction* means?

☐ place tourists visit ☐ rest stop
☐ unusual location

5. S-T-R-E-T-C-H: Is it true that very few people go to see this tilting tower? Cite text to support your claim.

Bats and Birds

Bats and birds have wings. Bats and birds are warm-blooded. That means they **generate** their own body heat unlike cold-blooded creatures such as reptiles. But here's a major difference. Bats have fur, while birds have feathers. And here's why. Bats aren't birds, but are mammals instead. That's right, bats are part of the same group of animals that includes mice, elephants, and humans. In fact, they even have hands. Their wings are actually skin that spreads between their five fingers. When a bat flies, you could say that it is flapping its hands. Wow, that's weird!

KEY QUESTIONS

Cite text for all questions except #4.

1. COMPARE: In the text, a similarity between bats and birds is: "_____."

2. CONTRAST: In the text, a difference between the two is: "_____."

3. FUN FIND: This sentence lists three animals bats are related to: "_____."

4. CONTEXT CLUES: What do you think *generate* means?

☐ make ☐ lose
☐ an army leader

5. S-T-R-E-T-C-H: Do birds and bats both have fur? Cite text to support your claim.

Copernicus, Ahead of His Time

Today we know that the sun is at the center of our solar system. All the planets, including Earth, orbit this star. But long ago, everyone believed that Earth was at the center. I think that idea is pretty funny. People thought that the sun and the other planets circled around Earth. In the 16th century a Polish scientist named Nicolaus Copernicus did not agree. He **opposed** this accepted idea. He wrote a book explaining that Earth actually rotated around the sun. At the time, people didn't believe Copernicus. They thought his idea was silly. It took many years before the world realized he was right. Copernicus was cool!

KEY QUESTIONS

Cite text for all questions except #4.

1. FACT: A fact in the text is: "_____."

2. OPINION: An opinion in the text is: "_____."

3. FUN FIND: Did people believe what Copernicus wrote? The author states, "_____."

4. CONTEXT CLUES: What do you think *opposed* means?

☐ disagreed with ☐ agreed with
☐ write about

5. S-T-R-E-T-C-H: How was Copernicus ahead of his time? Cite text to support your claim.

Ouch! Brain Freeze

Some call it *brain freeze*. Some call it *ice-cream headache*. But whatever you call it, it's not very pleasant. It's that **piercing** sensation you can get in your forehead when you eat something very cold, like ice cream or frozen yogurt. What causes brain freeze? When a very cold substance hits the roof of your mouth, blood flow increases. The increased blood flow triggers pain in the head. Not everyone experiences brain freeze when they eat something cold. But if you do, a sip of warm water will usually help the uncomfortable feeling pass.

KEY QUESTIONS

Cite text for all questions except #4.

1. CAUSE: What causes brain freeze? According to the text, "_____."

2. EFFECT: What is the effect of increased blood flow? The text says, "_____."

3. FUN FIND: What's another name for brain freeze? The author states, "_____."

4. CONTEXT CLUES: What do you think *piercing* means?

☐ funny ☐ loud ☐ sharp

5. S-T-R-E-T-C-H: Does everyone experience brain freeze when they eat something cold? Cite text to support your claim.

What a Place!

Santorini is one of the world's most gorgeous places. It is a Greek island in the Mediterranean Sea. On the island, there's a town built into the side of a cliff. You can get to the town by riding a donkey up a steep path. The houses there are beautiful—bright white with blue doors. At the beaches, the water is warm and calm. Some sand is black or red. That's because it's an unusual type of sand made by volcanoes.

Nothing compares to a **spectacular** Santorini sunset. As the sun sinks, bands of orange and pink form above the black sand and shining sea. What a place!

KEY QUESTIONS

Cite text for all questions except #4.

1. DESCRIPTION: A sentence that describes the location of Santorini is: "_____."

2. DESCRIPTION: A sentence that describes the beaches of Santorini is: "_____."

3. FUN FIND: A sentence that mentions an animal is: "_____."

4. CONTEXT CLUES: What do you think *spectacular* means?

☐ dramatically beautiful
☐ unpleasant-looking
☐ requiring eyeglasses

5. S-T-R-E-T-C-H: Would you like to go to Santorini? Cite text to support your claim.

Self-Driving Cars

Companies such as Google are busy experimenting with cars that use computers to drive themselves. There are some advantages. Someone could type an address into the computer, and the car would go directly there. While the car drove itself, people could read or play video games. Maybe kids could even travel by themselves in a self-driving car. But there are also some serious concerns. A car's computer might **overreact**. It might slam on the brakes for a little object like a tin can in the road. Sometimes computers crash and that could cause the car to crash. Experts have mixed opinions about whether the world of the future will be full of self-driving cars.

KEY QUESTIONS

Cite text for all questions except #4.

1. PRO: This sentence gives an advantage of self-driving cars: "_____."

2. CON: This sentence gives a disadvantage of self-driving cars: "_____."

3. FUN FIND: Find a sentence that mentions a company. According to the text, "_____."

4. CONTEXT CLUES: What do you think *overreact* means?

☐ respond too strongly
☐ ignore something ☐ melt away

5. S-T-R-E-T-C-H: Would you like to have a self-driving car? Cite text to support your claim.

Hey, You! Get Lost!

For many animals, predators are just a part of life. When it comes to dodging enemies, animals have a variety of strategies to say, "Keep away!" Take the puffer fish. When this small fish feels threatened, it gulps water and **inflates** its body so its predator can't eat it. The tiny bombardier beetle keeps attackers away by spraying a super-hot liquid from its rear. The liquid is so hot it burns the predators. The opossum has a neat trick when enemies are around. It plays dead! Its body appears as dead as a doornail. And that means predators will no longer be interested in eating it. Wow!

KEY QUESTIONS

Cite text for all questions except #4.

1. MAIN IDEA: A sentence that tells the main idea is: "_____."

2. DETAILS: What is an example of a self-defense strategy? According to the passage, "_____."

3. FUN FIND: A simile compares two unlike things using the word *like* or *as*. *As stubborn as a mule* is a simile. A sentence that includes a simile is: "_____."

4. CONTEXT CLUES: What do you think *inflates* means?

☐ dives ☐ shrinks ☐ blows up

5. S-T-R-E-T-C-H: Would you like to have a bombardier beetle as a pet? Cite text to support your claim.

TEXT EVIDENCE: INFORMATIONAL

LOUD SOUNDS!!!!!

Sounds can be loud or even **ear-splitting**. This can hurt your ears. Sound is measured in units called decibels. A quiet sound, such as a whisper, measures about 15 decibels. Conversation is at about 60 decibels. Sounds above 85 decibels can make your ears hurt, especially if you're exposed to them for a long time. For that reason, you should avoid situations where the sounds are too loud. But sometimes you may have no choice, such as when you go to a concert. A loud rock concert can reach 120 decibels. Earplugs are a must—don't forget them!

KEY QUESTIONS

Cite text for all questions except #4.

1. CAUSE: A sentence that states the cause is: "_____."

2. EFFECT: A sentence that states the effect is: "_____."

3. FUN FIND: How many decibels can a rock concert reach? According to the text, "_____."

4. CONTEXT CLUES: What do you think *ear-splitting* means?

☐ very soft   ☐ breakable   ☐ very loud

5. S-T-R-E-T-C-H: What does the author suggest you take to loud rock concerts? Cite text to support your claim.

TEXT EVIDENCE: INFORMATIONAL

Telling Sea Lions From Seals

Seals and sea lions are two of the most lovable creatures in the ocean. While these two mammals are similar, they are different animals. They both have big, blubbery bodies. Both have big dark eyes, long whiskers, and two sets of flippers. One difference is that sea lions can walk on land, but seals can't. Instead they move on land by **wriggling** on their bellies. The animals' ears are another clue to telling them apart. Seals have ear holes, but no ear flap. But sea lions' ears are covered with a small flap, like cats and dogs. Now you know how to tell them apart.

KEY QUESTIONS

Cite text for all questions except #4.

1. COMPARE: A sentence that tells how seals and sea lions are similar is: "_____."

2. CONTRAST: A sentence that tells how seals and sea lions are different is: "_____."

3. FUN FIND: Find an opinion in the passage? A sentence containing an opinion is: "_____."

4. CONTEXT CLUES: What do you think *wriggling* means?

☐ turning   ☐ swimming   ☐ wiggling

5. S-T-R-E-T-C-H: Do sea lions and seals each have three sets of flippers? Cite text to support your claim.

Haggis

Haggis is Scotland's national dish. It's a kind of pudding made from parts of a sheep's heart, liver, and lungs. Haggis does not sound tasty. But it's so popular in Scotland that you can buy haggis in the grocery store. During a national holiday called Burns Night, Scots dine on haggis. Burns Night is a celebration of a famous Scottish poet named Robert Burns. On this special day, people **recite** his poetry, play the bagpipes, and eat their national dish. Celebrating Burns Night would be fun. Well, the holiday would be fun if it weren't for the haggis.

KEY QUESTIONS

Cite text for all questions except #4.

1. FACT: Here's a fact in the text: "_____."

2. OPINION: Here's an opinion in the text: "_____."

3. FUN FIND: What is haggis made from? The text says, "_____."

4. CONTEXT CLUES: What do you think *recite* means?

☐ see again ☐ say aloud from memory
☐ eat again

5. S-T-R-E-T-C-H: Would you like to eat haggis? Cite text to support your claim.

The Making of Central Park

Even in the old days, New York City was big and busy. But there was a problem. New York City didn't have many open spaces where people could go to relax. What was the solution? Central Park was created. Thousands of trees were planted. Paths were laid out for people to walk on. A man-made lake was even dug and filled with water. The lake was perfect for row boating in summer and ice skating in winter. When it opened in 1858, Central Park quickly became a very popular spot. It still is today. If you go to New York, make sure to visit Central Park. Central Park is an **oasis** of calm in the crowded city.

KEY QUESTIONS

Cite text for all questions except #4.

1. PROBLEM: The problem in the text is: "_____."

2. SOLUTION: The solution in the text is: "_____."

3. FUN FIND: What was the lake perfect for? According to the text: "_____."

4. CONTEXT CLUES: What do you think *oasis* means?

☐ capital of Hawaii ☐ slang for "sister"
☐ calm spot

5. S-T-R-E-T-C-H: Why does the author say, "Central Park is an oasis of calm in the crowded city"? Cite text to support your claim.

Spectacular Fireflies

Fireflies are fabulous insects! Many people have never seen a firefly because they live only in certain parts of the country. Plus, fireflies also live for only a **brief** time each summer—usually between the months of June and August. Fireflies are actually a kind of beetle. The light they give off is the result of a chemical reaction called bioluminescence. The main purpose of the light is to attract a mate. Other names for fireflies are "glowworms" and "lightning bugs." But I think the name "firefly" says it best.

KEY QUESTIONS

Cite text for all questions except #4.

1. FACT: A fact in the text is:
"_____."

2. OPINION: An opinion in the text is:
"_____."

3. FUN FIND: This detail in the text is very interesting to me: "_____."

4. CONTEXT CLUES: What do you think *brief* means?

☐ short ☐ summer ☐ unusual

5. S-T-R-E-T-C-H: Can you think of a brand-new name for fireflies? Cite text to tell why you picked it.

School, Near and Far

What would it be like to go to school in Japan? In some ways, it wouldn't be much different. Japanese kids study math, social studies, and science, just like you. They have art and music and sometimes go on field trips. And they learn to read and write and do math. But there are a few differences, too. In the U.S., kids **attend** school for about 160 days, but Japanese kids go for about 240. American schools employ janitors to keep schools clean, but in Japan kids do some of the cleaning. They even wear special indoor shoes to keep things tidy!

KEY QUESTIONS

Cite text for all questions except #4.

1. COMPARE: A sentence that tells how school in Japan is similar to school here is: "_____."

2. CONTRAST: A sentence that tells how school in Japan is different is: "_____."

3. FUN FIND: How do Japanese students keep their school tidy? According to the text, "_____."

4. CONTEXT CLUES: What do you think *attend* means?

☐ go to ☐ study ☐ clean

5. S-T-R-E-T-C-H: Would you like to go to school in Japan? Cite text to support your claim.

A Very Long Bridge

The world's longest bridge is in China. It is called the Danyang-Kunshan Grand Bridge. Cars and people don't use the bridge. It is for high-speed trains. The bridge is 102 miles long. It **spans** a part of China where the land is low and swampy. Such land is perfect for growing rice so there are many rice farms here. In some places, the bridge stands 100 feet above the rice fields. It took four years and ten thousand construction workers to build the giant structure. The bridge opened in 2011. Do you know what that means? If you were born before that year, you are older than the world's longest bridge.

KEY QUESTIONS

Cite text for all questions except #4.

1. DETAILS: This sentence tells the name of the bridge: "_____."

2. DETAILS: This sentence gives its length: "_____."

3. FUN FIND: This sentence tells what kind of vehicle uses the bridge: "_____."

4. CONTEXT CLUES: What do you think *spans* means?

☐ departs ☐ crosses ☐ cleans

5. S-T-R-E-T-C-H: Do farmers grow wheat under the bridge? Cite text to support your claim.

Parachuting Beavers

Back in the 1950s, the state of Idaho had a problem—a furry, little problem to be exact. There were too many beavers living near people. The creatures soon became pests, building dams that stopped streams from flowing through cities and farms. How was the problem fixed? A plan was hatched to move the beavers to a better place. This required placing the creatures in special boxes. The boxes had airholes and parachutes attached. Workers loaded the live **cargo** onto airplanes. When the planes were high above the wilderness, workers dropped the boxes and the parachutes opened. Down floated the beavers to their new homes, deep in the woods and far away from people.

KEY QUESTIONS

Cite text for all questions except #4.

1. PROBLEM: According to the author, the problem is: "_____."

2. SOLUTION: According to the author, the solution is: "_____."

3. FUN FIND: This sentence describes the special boxes: "_____."

4. CONTEXT CLUES: What do you think *cargo* means?

☐ large airplane ☐ type of fish
☐ items carried in a vehicle

5. S-T-R-E-T-C-H: Did the beavers get moved to sunny beaches? Cite text to support your claim.

Dry, Dry, Droughts

Sometimes no rain falls for many weeks. A drought sets in. During a drought, the ground gets very dry. Plants may shrivel up or even die. Because there's less water, your community may create rules about how much you can use. A common way to save water is by not leaving the sink running the whole time you're brushing your teeth. That's wasteful. People can also take showers rather than baths. That's because showering uses  less water than taking a bath. When water is **scarce**, people have to find ways not to use so much.

KEY QUESTIONS

Cite text for all questions except #4.

1. CAUSE: A sentence that states the cause is: "_____."

2. EFFECT: A sentence that states the effect is: "_____."

3. FUN FIND: What can happen to plants during a drought? According to the text, "_____."

4. CONTEXT CLUES: What do you think *scarce* means?

☐ frightening ☐ wet ☐ rare

5. S-T-R-E-T-C-H: What is one way to save water during a drought? Cite text to support your claim.

Dogs: Paws Up or Paws Down?

 Some people think dogs are the best pets. Dogs have a well-deserved reputation for being friendly and loyal. Dogs enjoy spending time with people. They are smart animals and can learn tricks. But there are also **downsides** to dog ownership. Dogs require a lot of attention. They need to be walked. Dogs can be messy. They can track mud into your home. Dogs can also be loud. They might bother you or your neighbors with their barking. You'll have to decide whether or not a dog is the right pet for you. If not, there are so many other great pets to choose from. Consider a cat, bird, fish, hamster, or iguana.

KEY QUESTIONS

Cite text for all questions except #4.

1. PRO: This sentence states an advantage of dogs: "_____."

2. CON: This sentence states a disadvantage of dogs: "_____."

3. FUN FIND: This sentence lists some pets besides dogs: "_____."

4. CONTEXT CLUES: What do you think *downsides* means?

☐ effects ☐ disadvantages
☐ advantages

5. S-T-R-E-T-C-H: Would you like to have a dog for a pet? Why? Cite text to support your claim.

From Oswald to Elsa

Born in 1901, Walt Disney spent his childhood in the Midwest. As an adult, he built a gigantic entertainment empire. But it all started with Oswald, the Lucky Rabbit. Oswald was Walt Disney's first hit cartoon in 1927. The character, **rendered** in black and white, had black fur and long, floppy ears. Then, in 1928, Disney created Mickey Mouse. After Mickey came such memorable cartoon characters as Donald Duck, Pluto, and Goofy. Today, millions of people around the world view Disney movies. I think *Frozen* is the best Disney movie ever! Elsa is an amazing character. And the songs in *Frozen* are so fun to sing along to.

KEY QUESTIONS

Cite text for all questions except #4.

1. FACT: Here's a fact in the text: "_____."

2. OPINION: Here's an opinion in the text: "_____."

3. FUN FIND: Another opinion in the text is: "_____."

4. CONTEXT CLUES: What do you think *rendered* means?

☐ twisted ☐ drawn ☐ cartoonish

5. S-T-R-E-T-C-H: Is this author's favorite Disney movie *The Lion King*? Cite text to support your claim.

The Remarkable Rosa Parks

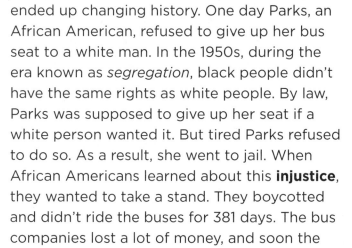

Rosa Parks was an ordinary woman who ended up changing history. One day Parks, an African American, refused to give up her bus seat to a white man. In the 1950s, during the era known as *segregation*, black people didn't have the same rights as white people. By law, Parks was supposed to give up her seat if a white person wanted it. But tired Parks refused to do so. As a result, she went to jail. When African Americans learned about this **injustice**, they wanted to take a stand. They boycotted and didn't ride the buses for 381 days. The bus companies lost a lot of money, and soon the segregation laws were changed.

KEY QUESTIONS

Cite text for all questions except #4.

1. MAIN IDEA: The sentence containing the main idea of this passage is, "_____."

2. DETAILS: What did Rosa Parks do one day that helped change history? According to the text, "_____."

3. FUN FIND: What effect did the bus boycott have? According to the text, "_____."

4. CONTEXT CLUES: What do you think *injustice* means?

☐ unfairness ☐ issue ☐ disagreement

5. S-T-R-E-T-C-H: Why is the title of this passage *The Remarkable Rosa Parks*? Cite text to support your claim.

Standing Tall When the Ground Shakes

During an earthquake, sections of the earth move and shake. Most earthquakes are so small people can't even feel them. Big earthquakes, however, can do a lot of damage. The big San Francisco earthquake in 1906 lasted less than a minute, but it caused hundreds of buildings to come crashing down. What was the solution? Engineers developed a process called "seismic retrofitting." Seismic retrofitting is when engineers add beams and columns made of concrete and steel to strengthen existing buildings. This makes them more sturdy, so they can **withstand** strong shakes. For cities, it's a lot cheaper and easier to retrofit buildings than to build brand-new ones.

KEY QUESTIONS

Cite text for all questions except #4.

1. PROBLEM: The problem in the text is, "_____ ."

2. SOLUTION: The solution in the text is, "_____ ."

3. FUN FIND: One detail in the text I found interesting is: "_____ ."

4. CONTEXT CLUES: What do you think *withstand* means?

☐ handle   ☐ remember   ☐ protect

5. S-T-R-E-T-C-H: Did architects develop the process of seismic retrofitting? Cite text to support your claim.

How to Make an Ice Cream Sundae—Any Day!

An ice cream sundae is a delicious treat you can make at home. It's as easy as pie! Here's how you do it. First, you get a bowl to hold the sundae. Next, you scoop in your favorite flavor of ice cream. You might even include two different flavors. Next **drizzle** on a flavored sauce, such as chocolate or caramel. You can then add some chopped nuts or strawberry slices—or whatever else you like. Finish your creation with a touch of whipped cream and a cherry on top. The very last step is eating your sundae. *Yum!*

KEY QUESTIONS

Cite text for all questions except #4.

1. SEQUENCE: What is the first step in making an ice cream sundae? The author states, "_____."

2. SEQUENCE: What is the second step? The author states, "_____."

3. FUN FIND: A simile compares two unlike things using the word *like* or *as*. As *stubborn as a mule* is a simile. A sentence that contains a simile is: "_____."

4. CONTEXT CLUES: What do you think *drizzle* means?

☐ pour lightly   ☐ whip   ☐ spoon

5. S-T-R-E-T-C-H: Is putting a cherry on top of a sundae the very last step? Cite text to support your claim.

The Phases of the Moon

Some nights you look up at the moon and see a big round ball. Other times, it's only a thin sliver. And sometimes you can't see the moon at all. These differences in the moon's **appearance** are called the moon's phases. But what causes these phases? The reason the moon always looks different is because its position is always changing. As it moves around Earth every 27 days, we see it from different angles. It's the different positions in the moon's orbit that change its appearance here on Earth.

KEY QUESTIONS

Cite text for all questions except #4.

1. CAUSE: What causes the differences in the moon's appearance? According to the text, "_____."

2. EFFECT: What effect does the moon's orbit have on its appearance here on Earth? According to the text, "_____."

3. FUN FIND: Can you find a sentence that compares the moon to a toy? The text says, "_____."

4. CONTEXT CLUES: What do you think *appearance* means?

☐ how something moves
☐ how something looks
☐ how something sounds

5. S-T-R-E-T-C-H: Are there times when the moon is not visible? Cite text to support your claim.

Narwhals: Unicorns of the Sea

Unicorns are horselike creatures with a single horn coming out of their heads. But unicorns are mythical, which means they don't really exist. While there aren't really unicorns roaming the earth, there *are* unicorns living in the sea. A narwhal is a type of whale that is sometimes called a "sea unicorn." Narwhals have a long horn **protruding** from their head. This horn is spiraled and can be up to ten feet long. Fully grown narwhals can reach 3,000 pounds. They live in the cold waters of the Arctic Circle.

KEY QUESTIONS

Cite text for all questions except #4.

1. DETAILS: A sentence that tells how much fully grown narwhals weigh is: "_____."

2. DETAILS: A sentence that tells the length of a narwhal's horn is: "_____."

3. FUN FIND: Can you find a sentence that tells whether unicorns are real? The author states, "_____."

4. CONTEXT CLUES: What do you think *protruding* means?

☐ make believe
☐ sticking out
☐ spiraled

5. S-T-R-E-T-C-H: Why are narwhals called *sea unicorns*? Cite text to support your claim.

Aloha, Hawaii!

Hawaii is an amazing place. In 1959, it became America's fiftieth state. But Hawaii isn't a landlocked state like Iowa, Illinois, or Indiana. Hawaii is an island in the middle of the Pacific Ocean. It's about halfway between California and Japan. And Hawaii doesn't **consist** of just one island, either. The state is a group of 132 islands. There are eight main islands, including Maui and Oahu. The island of Oahu is the location of Hawaii's capital city, Honolulu. With its palm trees and beaches, it's a great place to visit. But if you visit Oahu, just think, you still have 131 other islands to explore.

KEY QUESTIONS

Cite text for all questions except #4.

1. MAIN IDEA: A sentence that includes the main idea in this text is: "_____."

2. DETAILS: A sentence with a detail is: "_____."

3. FUN FIND: Alliteration is a sequence of words that start with the same letter, such as "dance, dip, and dive." This sentence contains alliteration: "_____."

4. CONTEXT CLUES: What do you think *consist* means?

☐ to be made of ☐ constantly
☐ to get angry at

5. S-T-R-E-T-C-H: Is Hawaii about halfway between Florida and Australia? Cite text to support your claim.

Should We Raise the Driving Age to 18?

The driving age is 16 in most states in America. Is that too young . . . or just right? Some people think it's too young. They say that driving a car is a big responsibility and 16-year-olds can be careless. Younger teens are more likely to be texting when they should be watching the road, they say. By 18, teens are more responsible. But others think that 16 is the **appropriate** age to drive. These people think age isn't the issue.  Practice and experience are what really count. The important thing is making sure 16-year-olds have a gazillion hours of practice before they get their license. What do *you* think?

KEY QUESTIONS

Cite text for all questions except #4.

1. PRO: A sentence that argues in favor of raising the driving age is: "_____."

2. CON: A sentence that argues against raising the driving age is: "_____."

3. FUN FIND: A hyperbole is an extreme exaggeration, such as *older than the hills*. A sentence that contains a hyperbole is: "_____."

4. CONTEXT CLUES: What do you think *appropriate* means?

☐ fancy ☐ right ☐ young

5. S-T-R-E-T-C-H: Do you think the driving age should be raised to 18? Cite text to support your claim.

Umbrellas Are Also for Fellas

In a rainstorm, you can easily get extremely wet. The umbrella was created to help a person stay dry. It was invented in the country of China. The first ones appeared nearly 3,000 years ago. Soon the invention spread to ancient Rome and Greece. At first, however, umbrellas were only used by women. Then, an Englishman named Jonas Hanway started using an umbrella in the 1700s. He was a famous **merchant** so other men followed his example. These days, umbrellas are for everyone: men and women, young and old. So, let it rain!

KEY QUESTIONS

Cite text for all questions except #4.

1. PROBLEM: The problem in the text is: "_____."

2. SOLUTION: The solution in the text is: "_____."

3. FUN FIND: Where was the umbrella invented? According to the text, "_____."

4. CONTEXT CLUES: What do you think *merchant* means?

☐ painter ☐ business person
☐ person with fins

5. S-T-R-E-T-C-H: Why is *Umbrellas Are Also for Fellas* a good title for this passage? Cite text to support your claim.

Horses, Of Course!

Giddy up! It's time to learn about horses. Foals are usually born at night. These "baby horses" learn to walk when they are just a few hours old. They fall down a lot! At first, foals only drink milk from their mothers. But within a month, they begin to nibble grass and hay. As they grow, they love to munch treats like carrots, apples, and sugar cubes. Horses don't eat any meat, which makes them **herbivores**. At three years of age, a horse is considered all grown-up. Adult females are called mares and adult males are called stallions. Some stallions weigh 700 pounds or more. Adult horses can trot, run, and jump. They can also take you for a ride. *Yeehaw!*

KEY QUESTIONS

Cite text for all questions except #4.

1. DETAILS: A sentence that tells when baby horses are born is: "_____."

2. DETAILS: A sentence that tells how much a horse can weigh is: "_____."

3. FUN FIND: A cowboy word at the very end of the passage is: "_____!"

4. CONTEXT CLUES: What do you think *herbivores* means?

☐ meat eaters
☐ plant eaters
☐ pizza eaters

5. S-T-R-E-T-C-H: Do horses eat a lot of meat? Cite text to support your claim.

Rain Forest Fashion

It was Cindy's summer vacation. Her family was on a visit to the Amazon rain forest. Cindy wore jeans and a white T-shirt. She spotted a butterfly. It was an incredible shade of blue. A bird flew by. Its feathers were every color of the rainbow. She saw a waterfall. It glistened like white diamonds. Wow! Cindy was **gobsmacked**. After a day of hiking in nature, Cindy's family visited a souvenir shop. Cindy picked out the most brightly colored T-shirt in the store. It was neon pink with sequins and glitter.

"Why that shirt?" asked her brother.

"The rain forest inspired me to really stand out," said Cindy with a giggle.

KEY QUESTIONS

Cite text for all questions except #4.

1. SETTING: A sentence that tells where this story takes place is, "_____."

2. SETTING: A sentence that tells when this story takes place is, "_____."

3. FUN FIND: According to the story, this is what Cindy did at the shop: "_____."

4. CONTEXT CLUES: What do you think *gobsmacked* means?

☐ amazed ☐ bored ☐ hot

5. S-T-R-E-T-C-H: Did Cindy wear shorts and a red T-shirt to hike in the Amazon? Cite text to support your claim.

Trudy Spills the Beans

"Can you keep a secret?" Trudy's older sister asked. Six-year-old Trudy loved secrets. Her favorite part about secrets was sharing them! "You can't tell Mom," her sister said. Trudy promised, and so her sister told her: On Sunday, Dad was taking them for a ride in a hot-air balloon. The balloon ride was a surprise for Mom's birthday. When Sunday came, Dad packed a lunch, pretending they were going for a picnic. As they were leaving, Mom told everyone, "Bring sweaters because it might be cold up in the balloon." Everyone looked at Trudy. "Oops!" she said, blushing. "I guess I'm not very good at keeping secrets."

KEY QUESTIONS

Cite text for all questions except #4.

1. INFERENCE: The sentence that shows that Mom knows about the secret is: "_____."

2. INFERENCE: The sentence that shows everyone knows it was Trudy who told Mom is: "_____."

3. FUN FIND: What is Trudy's favorite part about secrets? The text says, "_____."

4. CONTEXT CLUES: What do you think the saying *spills the beans* means?

☐ drops something
☐ tells a secret ☐ forgets a sweater

5. S-T-R-E-T-C-H: Why is the story called *Trudy Spills the Beans*? Cite text to support your claim.

Knock Knack Noah

Noah's alarm rang. As he turned it off, he knocked the clock off his table. At breakfast, he spilled his orange juice. Noah was great at being clumsy. You could say he had a **knack** for knocking things over. When he arrived at school, he bumped into a row of bikes. They tipped over, one by one, like a line of dominoes. During class, he toppled a tall stack of books. After school, Noah went bowling. He rolled the ball, and it knocked down all the pins. Strike! He did it again—another strike! Indeed, Noah had a knack for knocking things over.

KEY QUESTIONS

Cite text for all questions except #4.

1. CHARACTER: A sentence that describes a character trait of Noah's is: "_____."

2. CHARACTER: A sentence that tells you what Noah had a knack for is: "_____."

3. FUN FIND: This sentence tells what happened when Noah bumped the bikes: "_____."

4. CONTEXT CLUES: What do you think *knack* means?

☐ backpack ☐ mistake ☐ talent

5. S-T-R-E-T-C-H: What sport does Noah have a special talent for? Cite text to support your claim.

Identical . . . Not!

Mia and Alice were identical twins. They were the same height and had the same haircut. They both loved fifth grade. But they were also very different. Unlike Alice, Mia loved books, puzzles, and games. She was a chess fanatic! In contrast, Alice's passion was sports: soccer, basketball, and long bike rides. The more **strenuous** the better! What was the sisters' very favorite activity to do together? They both LOVED going to the movies and sitting side by side. And every Saturday afternoon, that's exactly what they did! They always shared popcorn with extra butter, and they always had a blast.

KEY QUESTIONS

Cite text for all questions except #4.

1. COMPARE: A sentence that shows how the sisters are similar is: "_____."

2. CONTRAST: A sentence that shows how the sisters are different is: "_____."

3. FUN FIND: What was the sisters' very favorite activity to do together? According to the story, "_____."

4. CONTEXT CLUES: What do you think *strenuous* means?

☐ easy and fun ☐ nice and friendly
☐ hard and tiring

5. S-T-R-E-T-C-H: Which sister are you more like, Mia or Alice? Cite text to support your claim.

Felix Goes Fishing

Felix was excited. He and his family were off on a three-hour fishing **expedition**! The man leading the trip asked if any of the passengers had gone fishing before. Felix's two older brothers bragged they were great at fishing, even though they had never done it before. But Felix admitted that he didn't know how to fish. Honesty is the best policy. The man gave Felix lots of pointers. He showed Felix how to put bait on the hook. He showed him how to cast his fishing line. During the expedition, Felix's

brothers didn't catch any fish. Felix, however, caught three humongous sea bass. Felix, the young fisherman, really made a splash!

KEY QUESTIONS

Cite text for all questions except #4.

1. THEME: A sentence that states the main theme of the story is: "_____."

2. THEME: Here's a sentence that shows how Felix was rewarded for telling the truth: "_____."

3. FUN FIND: This sentence tells how long the fishing trip lasted: "_____."

4. CONTEXT CLUES: What do you think *expedition* means?

☐ a long nap ☐ a big tent
☐ a group trip

5. S-T-R-E-T-C-H: Why is honesty the best policy? Cite text to support your claim.

Spooked

Sherman walked down Walnut Street in his Batman costume. He looked at all the spooky decorations—cobwebs and skeletons and jack-o'-lanterns glowing with **sinister** grins. Sherman rang the next doorbell. "Trick or treat!" he said, and received two pieces of candy. As he walked back to the sidewalk, he noticed a skeleton lying in a coffin, which gave him the creeps. Suddenly he felt a hand on his shoulder. When he turned, he was looking into the face of a zombie. "Aaaa!" Sherman screamed, dropping his bag of candy. The zombie lifted his rubber mask, and there was Jamal, Sherman's best pal. "I knew it was you the whole time," said a very relieved Sherman.

KEY QUESTIONS

Cite text for all questions except #4.

1. SETTING: A sentence that tells where this story is set is: "_____."

2. SETTING: The story takes place on Halloween. A sentence that shows this is, "_____."

3. FUN FIND: What does Sherman see that makes him scream? According to the story, "_____."

4. CONTEXT CLUES: What do you think *sinister* means?

☐ mean ☐ happy ☐ bright

5. S-T-R-E-T-C-H: Do you believe that Sherman *really* knew it was Jamal in the zombie costume? Cite text to support your claim.

That's NOT How You Do It!

Avery's bossy cousin Stella came for a visit. Cranky Stella was always **glowering**. The girls sat in the kitchen sketching. Avery drew a ship on a stormy sea. "That's NOT how you draw a ship!" Stella said. Avery just smiled. When Avery told Stella her favorite joke, Stella said, "That's NOT how you tell a joke." Avery just smiled. Later, they went outside to shoot hoops. Avery shot and the ball bounced off the rim and went in. Stella grabbed the ball and said, "That's NOT how you shoot a basket!" But then Stella shot and missed. Avery smiled a very big smile.

KEY QUESTIONS

Cite text for all questions except #4.

1. CHARACTER: A sentence that describes Stella's personality is: "_____."

2. CHARACTER: A sentence that describes Stella's appearance is: "_____."

3. FUN FIND: What picture does Avery draw? According to the story, "_____."

4. CONTEXT CLUES: What do you think *glowering* means?

☐ smiling   ☐ laughing   ☐ frowning

5. S-T-R-E-T-C-H: What event makes Avery smile at the end of the story? Why? Cite text to support your claim.

Freshly Fallen Snowman

It was late December. Simone was excited to build a snowman. She gave it radishes for eyes, a carrot for a nose, and sticks for arms. It looked great, but Simone felt her snowman still needed something. She **furnished** a hat and scarf. But she felt her snowman still needed something. She placed winter gloves on the end of its stick arms. The heavy gloves caused the sticks to break off, and the whole snowman came tumbling down. Simone quickly grasped what had gone wrong. You should leave well enough alone. Simone made a new snowman featuring radishes, carrots, sticks, and everything but the gloves. It was just right.

KEY QUESTIONS

Cite text for all questions except #4.

1. THEME: A sentence that states the theme of the story is: "_____."

2. THEME: This sentence describes the new snowman Simone built: "_____."

3. FUN FIND: When is this story set? The text states, "_____."

4. CONTEXT CLUES: What do you think *furnished* means?

☐ an oven   ☐ provided   ☐ took away

5. S-T-R-E-T-C-H: Why is *Freshly Fallen Snowman* a good title for this story? Cite text to support your claim.

Lemonade for Ice Cream

Jackie and her brother Jason wanted to buy ice cream cones, but they didn't have any money. Jackie had an idea. "Let's pick the lemons from the tree out back and make some lemonade to sell." They made two big pitchers and sold it out on the sidewalk. It was so hot that lots of people stopped to buy their lemonade. Some people even bought two glasses! **In no time flat**, they were all out of lemonade. Jackie's idea worked. They earned enough money by selling lemonade to buy two ice cream cones. Two mint-chip-mango-pecan-caramel-twirl ice cream cones to be exact. *Yum!*

KEY QUESTIONS

Cite text for all questions except #4.

1. CONFLICT: A sentence that shows the conflict is: "_____."

2. RESOLUTION: The sentence that shows the resolution is: "_____."

3. FUN FIND: Whose idea is it to sell lemonade? The story says, "_____."

4. CONTEXT CLUES: What do you think the saying *in no time flat* means?

☐ eventually ☐ never ☐ very quickly

5. S-T-R-E-T-C-H: Did the kids make three pitchers of lemonade? Cite text to support your claim.

Thoughtful Theo

Theo sat on the park bench with his mom. He was eating a peanut butter sandwich she made. There were pigeons all around. Theo took tiny bites and made a face. He set down his partly eaten sandwich on a paper lunch bag. Soon pigeons began to peck at it. "Oh no!" said Theo, **feigning** surprise. "I can't eat it now."

"Let's go home, and I'll make you a new one," said his mom.

"That's one idea," said Theo with a sly smile. "May I suggest another? There's an ice cream truck right over there. Buying me a mint-chip cone would be so much more convenient for you."

"You are *always* so thoughtful," she replied with a wink. Then Theo's mom reached for her wallet.

KEY QUESTIONS

Cite text for all questions except #4.

1. INFERENCE: This sentence shows that Theo doesn't want his sandwich: "_____."

2. INFERENCE: This sentence shows that Theo's mom will get his ice cream: "_____."

3. FUN FIND: When Theo set down his sandwich, here's what happened: "_____."

4. CONTEXT CLUES: What do you think *feigning* means?

☐ sighing ☐ passing out
☐ pretending

5. S-T-R-E-T-C-H: Were Theo and his mom sitting on a picnic blanket? Cite text to support your claim.

Quentin's Rough Start

Beep, beep, beep went the annoying alarm clock. Quentin was so tired. *This is the worst morning ever*, he thought. *Grrrrr.* When he went into the kitchen, there was no more of his favorite cereal. When he went back to his room to get dressed, he couldn't find his favorite pants. Or his shoes. Or his comb. And his hair was going in five different directions. He grabbed his book bag and prepared himself. This day was going to be **disastrous**. But then, his mom said, "Quentin, where are you going? It's Saturday!" *Saturday?* Suddenly his day was looking much better!

KEY QUESTIONS

Cite text for all questions except #4.

1. CHARACTER: A sentence that shows what Quentin thought about his morning is, "_____."

2. INFERENCE: A sentence that shows things aren't going well for Quentin is, "_____."

3. FUN FIND: An *onomatopoeia* is a word that sounds like its meaning, such as *zoom*. A sentence that contains an onomatopoeia is "_____."

4. CONTEXT CLUES: What do you think *disastrous* means?

☐ really funny ☐ really long
☐ really bad

5. S-T-R-E-T-C-H: Does the story end happily or unhappily? Cite text to support your claim.

Ruby and Ro

Ruby and Ro were both great at basketball. Both played on the Lions. While Ruby was a smooth and **adept** passer, Ro was a super shot. It was the league finals. The  score was tied, and the Tigers had the ball. Time was running out. Ruby made a great pass to Ro. Ro jumped, spun in the air, and shot. It was a basket at the buzzer. The Lions won!

"That was amazing," shouted someone in the crowd.

But Ro knew how much credit Ruby deserved.

"Thanks," said Ro. "I wouldn't have made that basket if Ruby hadn't passed it to me first."

KEY QUESTIONS

Cite text for all questions except #4.

1. COMPARE: A sentence that shows similarity in the story is: "_____."

2. CONTRAST: A sentence that shows difference in the story is: "_____."

3. FUN FIND: Which team won the game? According to the story, "_____."

4. CONTEXT CLUES: What do you think *adept* means?

☐ clumsy ☐ funny ☐ skilled

5. S-T-R-E-T-C-H: Does Ro appreciate Ruby's basketball skills? Cite text to support your claim.

Felipe vs. the Broccoli Spear

Felipe sat at the dinner table, arms folded across his chest, scowling at the spear of broccoli on his plate. Tonight it was broccoli, but some nights it was spinach or, even worse, kale! He had one big problem in life: Felipe **detested** green vegetables. Every night they were on his plate, and every night he couldn't eat them. "Just one piece," his mom said. And then Felipe got an idea. He loved hot sauce. He loved it on eggs, on pizza, even on popcorn. So he sprinkled a bit of hot sauce on his broccoli spear, and it was pretty tasty! "Could I have another?" he asked his mom.

KEY QUESTIONS

Cite text for all questions except #4.

1. CONFLICT: A sentence that shows the main conflict is, "_____."

2. RESOLUTION: A sentence that shows the resolution is, "_____."

3. FUN FIND: What other foods does Felipe like hot sauce on? According to the story, "_____."

4. CONTEXT CLUES: What do you think *detested* means?

☐ loved ☐ hated ☐ ate

5. S-T-R-E-T-C-H: Does Felipe like kale more than broccoli? Cite text to support your claim.

"That's fine."

At recess, the kids were choosing teams to play capture the flag. Lisa was the very last kid picked. "That's fine," she said.

Lisa looked away and quickly blinked back some tears. Renata, one of the other kids, was **distressed** to see Lisa so upset. During the game, Renata ran up beside Lisa. "It's my turn to be team captain next," said Renata. "I'm going to pick you first."

"That's fine," said Lisa. This time she broke into a big, happy grin.

KEY QUESTIONS

Cite text for all questions except #4.

1. INFERENCE: This sentence shows how Lisa feels when she's picked last: "_____."

2. INFERENCE: This sentence shows how Lisa feels when Renata says she'll pick her first: "_____."

3. FUN FIND: This sentence tells you what game the kids were playing: "_____."

4. CONTEXT CLUES: What do you think *distressed* means?

☐ faded jeans ☐ joyful ☐ unhappy

5. S-T-R-E-T-C-H: Who cares about Lisa's feelings? How do you know? Cite text to support your claim.

Akimi's Brother

Akimi thought her older brother was the nicest brother ever. Of course, he wasn't perfect. Sometimes he rolled his eyes at her jokes. And he thought her taste in music was **dreadful**. But when push came to shove, he was a good guy. On Halloween, when Akimi was too sick to go trick-or-treating, he shared all his candy with her. Another time, when they were walking and he found a twenty-dollar bill, he split the money with her. Akimi felt so lucky to have such an awesome brother. So, she used that ten dollars to buy him a ticket to the new superhero movie. Super indeed!

KEY QUESTIONS

Cite text for all questions except #4.

1. CHARACTER: A sentence that shows what Akimi's brother is like is: "_____."

2. CHARACTER: A sentence that shows how Akimi feels about her brother is: "_____."

3. FUN FIND: A sentence that shows how Akimi's brother isn't perfect is: "_____."

4. CONTEXT CLUES: What do you think *dreadful* means?

☐ funny ☐ great ☐ terrible

5. S-T-R-E-T-C-H: Does Akimi's brother always like her jokes? Cite text to support your claim.

Big Mess Challenge

Leo and Malik were on a TV show called *Big Mess Challenge*. The two were the finalists. First they had to slither through a mud pit. Both were equally good at slithering. So they came out of the mud pit tied. Next, they had to swing on a rope through a ketchup waterfall. Leo swang better than Malik. Now Leo was ahead in the challenge. Finally, they had to roll down a hill covered in cheese curls. Leo rolled better than Malik. Not surprisingly, Leo was the **victor**, and Malik came in second. Leo had mud, ketchup, and crushed-up cheese curls all over himself. "Congratulations," said the show's host. "You've won this brand new bar of soap."

KEY QUESTIONS

Cite text for all questions except #4.

1. COMPARE: A sentence that shows how Malik and Leo are similar is: "_____."

2. CONTRAST: A sentence that shows how they are different is: "_____."

3. FUN FIND: How did the winner of the challenge look? According to the text, "_____."

4. CONTEXT CLUES: What do you think *victor* means?

☐ winner ☐ loser ☐ quitter

5. S-T-R-E-T-C-H: Does the Big Mess Challenge include mustard, ketchup, or pickles? Cite text to support your claim.

A Movie Muddle

Diya couldn't decide which friend to take to the movies. For her birthday, she received a gift card worth two movie admissions. But she wasn't sure whether to take Mila or Angel. Whichever friend she took, the other was sure to be jealous and **cross**. But then Diya remembered something: Her grandma had sent twenty dollars for her birthday. By using the gift card and the money, Diya could take both friends. And they'd even have a few dollars left over for popcorn! Now, if only she could figure out which movie to see.

KEY QUESTIONS

Cite text for all questions except #4.

1. CONFLICT: A sentence that shows this story's conflict is: "_____."

2. RESOLUTION: A sentence that shows the resolution is: "_____."

3. FUN FIND: How much money did Diya's grandma send her? According to the story, "_____."

4. CONTEXT CLUES: What do you think *cross* means?

☐ ill ☐ happy ☐ angry

5. S-T-R-E-T-C-H: Will Diya have extra money to buy a treat at the movies? Cite text to support your claim.

Marta's Missing Tooth

On her way home from school, Marta's tooth fell out. She placed the tooth in her jacket pocket and hurried home. When she saw her grandmother, she smiled proudly, **revealing** the gap in her smile. But when she reached into her pocket, she got a terrible surprise. The tooth was lost! Marta soon realized what had happened. There was a hole in her pocket. Marta and her grandmother slowly retraced

her steps back to school. Before long, Marta spotted something like a white pebble on the sidewalk. "My tooth!" she said. Her smile was a mile wide.

KEY QUESTIONS

Cite text for all questions except #4.

1. CAUSE: What causes Marta's tooth to get lost? According to the story, "_____."

2. EFFECT: What is the effect of having a hole in her pocket? According to the story, "_____."

3. FUN FIND: A hyperbole is an extreme exaggeration, such as *older than the hills*. A sentence that contains a hyperbole is: "_____."

4. CONTEXT CLUES: What do you think *revealing* means?

☐ opening ☐ showing ☐ grinning

5. S-T-R-E-T-C-H: How does Marta feel about having a gap in her smile? Cite text to support your claim.

Strange Sounds

Milo was sleeping over at a friend's house. Once the lights were turned off, his friend's room felt so dark and unfamiliar. What was that strange tap, tap, tapping? What was that odd, tinkling music? Milo lay awake, his eyes wide as saucers. He pulled the sheets up to his chin. Finally, he couldn't stand it any more. He poked his sleeping friend on the shoulder.

"What is that t-t-tapping?" he asked fearfully, "and where is the weird music coming from?"

"It's raining," Milo's friend explained. "That's what is making the tapping sound. And the music is from the wind chimes on the porch."

Milo felt better. Now that he knew what the sounds were, the raindrops and wind chimes became **soothing**. He drifted off to sleep.

KEY QUESTIONS

Cite text for all questions except #4.

1. TONE: This story has a spooky tone. A sentence that shows this spooky tone is: "_____."

2. TONE: The story ends with a relieved tone. A sentence that shows this relieved tone is: "_____."

3. FUN FIND: When Milo got really scared, this is how he woke up his friend: "_____."

4. CONTEXT CLUES: What do you think *soothing* means?

☐ frightening ☐ interesting
☐ calming

5. S-T-R-E-T-C-H: At the very end of the story, does Milo eat milk and cookies? Cite text to support your claim.

Unplugged Saturday

Lexi's mom announced that today was Unplugged Saturday. Unplugged Saturday meant no TV, no video games, and no computer for the whole day. "No fair!" cried Lexi. She thought this was going to be the most boring day of her entire life. For a while, she **sulked** in her room. Then she went to see what her little brother was up to. He was building a fort in the backyard. "Want to help?" he asked. They spent the whole day building the coolest fort ever. Lexi had a blast! She never would have had this much fun with her brother if it hadn't been for Unplugged Saturday!

KEY QUESTIONS

Cite text for all questions except #4.

1. CHARACTER: One sentence that shows Lexi is unhappy about Unplugged Saturday is, "_____."

2. CHARACTER: A sentence that shows that Lexi changes her mind is, "_____."

3. FUN FIND: What is Unplugged Saturday? According to the story, "_____."

4. CONTEXT CLUES: What do you think *sulked* means?

☐ felt afraid ☐ felt sad ☐ felt happy

5. S-T-R-E-T-C-H: Does Lexi end up enjoying Unplugged Saturday? Cite text to support your claim.

Learning the Rules

Grady was very greedy. Whenever he had a little of something, he wanted a lot. One day, he joined some kids at school in playing a board game. It was called Zilcho. Grady had never played it before. The **object** was to get rid of all your cards. The first to do so was the winner. But Grady didn't listen to the rules. Every chance he had, Grady snatched cards until he had a tall pile. "I have the most cards," he announced proudly.

"You sure do," said one of the other kids. "That means you lose."

So Grady learned the game's rules. He also learned to be less greedy.

KEY QUESTIONS

Cite text for all questions except #4.

1. CHARACTER: A sentence that describes a character trait of Grady's personality is: "_____."

2. CHARACTER: A sentence that tells you the name of the board game is: "_____."

3. FUN FIND: How often had Grady played the game? The story says, "_____."

4. CONTEXT CLUES: What do you think *object* means?

☐ spacecraft ☐ fun ☐ goal

5. S-T-R-E-T-C-H: What two lessons does Grady learn at the end of this story? Cite text to support your claim.

Ears, the Rabbit

It was April 17th—also known as Min's birthday. She and her dad arrived at the pet store just as it was opening. Min had been to the shop several times, so she knew which rabbit she wanted—the gray one with the white nose. She ran to the rabbit cages, but her rabbit was gone! The shopkeeper told them that someone had taken it home the day before. Min was crushed. But then she spotted a rabbit she hadn't seen before. The bunny was brown with long **droopy** ears. He was as cute as a button! She liked this one even more than the gray one. And she already had a name for it: *Ears*.

KEY QUESTIONS

Cite text for all questions except #4.

1. SETTING: A sentence that shows where the story takes place is: "_____."

2. SETTING: A sentence that shows what day the story takes place is: "_____."

3. FUN FIND: A simile compares two unlike things using the word *like* or *as*. *As stubborn as a mule* is a simile. A sentence with a simile is: "_____."

4. CONTEXT CLUES: What do you think *droopy* means?

☐ hanging ☐ lonely ☐ pointed

5. S-T-R-E-T-C-H: Why does Min choose the name Ears for her rabbit? Cite text to support your claim.

Paint Problems

Lin's parents asked her to help paint chairs for the dining room table. She chose bright orange for hers. After a while, they took a break to eat lunch. Lin grabbed her meal and sat down. Oh no! She got wet paint on her pants. Lin went to her room and changed. Her friend called, and they talked for twenty minutes. Then Lin returned to finish her food. Oh no! She'd sat on wet paint again! That's when a big **realization** hit her: Learn from your mistakes. Lin changed once more. She finished her lunch on the stairs to make sure she didn't sit in paint again. Once the paint dried, the chair looked awesome. So Lin's parents let her paint the whole room bright orange.

KEY QUESTIONS

Cite text for all questions except #4.

1. THEME: A sentence that states the theme of the story is: "_____."

2. THEME: Lin did this to keep from making the mistake a third time: "_____."

3. FUN FIND: According to the story, here's how the chair looked in the end: "_____."

4. CONTEXT CLUES: What do you think *realization* means?

☐ anger ☐ confusion
☐ understanding

5. S-T-R-E-T-C-H: Does Lin paint her chair purple? Cite text to support your claim.

Otto Makes a Break for It

Otto the Octopus had been living for three years at the aquarium. He didn't mind living in his glass tank, but he missed the ocean, where he used to live. He longed to stretch his legs—all eight of them—and swim in the cool waters of the sea. After some thought, he decided to **make a break for it**. At night, when the aquarium workers had gone home, he nudged the top off his tank. Then he jumped to the ground. He slithered over to the drainpipe and slid down it. Just as he'd hoped, the pipe led him back to the sea. He was home at last!

KEY QUESTIONS

Cite text for all questions except #4.

1. SETTING: This sentence tells where the story takes place: "_____."

2. SETTING: A sentence that shows when this story takes place is: "_____."

3. FUN FIND: Why does Otto want to leave the aquarium? The story states, "_____."

4. CONTEXT CLUES: What do you think the saying *make a break for it* means?

☐ break something ☐ hide
☐ run away

5. S-T-R-E-T-C-H: What place does Otto consider home? Cite text to support your claim.

TEXT EVIDENCE: LITERARY

On Your Mark, Get Set . . . Stop!

Malika was the fastest runner on the track team. She had trained herself to be a fierce competitor. All Malika had to hear was the command to start a race: *On your mark, get set, go!* Then she'd run as fast as her two legs could carry her. One day, Malika stood in the hallway waiting for class to begin. Suddenly, a kid nearby told another kid to go find their friend. "Mark. Get Seth. Go!" he said.

When Malika heard this, she took off like a flash. But after about ten quick **strides**, she realized what had actually been said. What happened next? She stopped running and started laughing.

KEY QUESTIONS

Cite text for all questions except #4.

1. CAUSE: A sentence that states the cause is: "_____."

2. EFFECT: A sentence that states the effect is: "_____."

3. FUN FIND: This is what happened when Malika realized what had actually been said: "_____."

4. CONTEXT CLUES: What do you think *strides* means?

☐ short hops ☐ long steps
☐ cartwheels

5. S-T-R-E-T-C-H: Who is the fastest runner on the track team? Cite text to support your claim.

TEXT EVIDENCE: LITERARY

The Star

My name is Clive. Maybe you've heard about me. I was the star of the school play last year, and I was *amazing*. Some kids think I'm stuck on myself. But can I help it if I'm so much more talented than they are? My acting skills are stellar, and I just have a natural star quality. For some reason, the drama teacher gave me a smaller role this year. Actually, I'm playing a tree. I don't even have any lines. Some people might feel **slighted** to be given such a tiny part. But even in my small role, people will see what a star I am!

KEY QUESTIONS

Cite text for all questions except #4.

1. TONE: A sentence that shows that the tone of this story is boastful is, "_____."

2. CHARACTER: A sentence that shows how Clive's classmates view him is: "_____."

3. FUN FIND: What is Clive playing in this year's play? Clive says, "_____."

4. CONTEXT CLUES: What do you think *slighted* means?

☐ insulted ☐ confused ☐ happy

5. S-T-R-E-T-C-H: Does Clive have a lot of lines in the play? Cite text to support your claim.

The Cat in the House

I'm a dog. I like to dig holes, chase balls, paw through the trash, and chew socks. But the cat who lives here is such a bore. Does he bark? No, he meows and purrs! So **pathetic**! His idea of a good time is to lie around all day. And what's really maddening is that he hogs the sunniest spot in the house. He's so irritating. At night, when I'm trying to sleep, he races around like a maniac. I don't know how humans can stand such a pest. They don't get mad at him. They even seem to like him! Whenever

 I chase him, they say, "Poor kitty" and "Bad dog!" That cat is sooooo annoying!

KEY QUESTIONS

Cite text for all questions except #4.

1. TONE: The tone of this story is grumpy. A sentence that shows the grumpy tone is, "_____."

2. INFERENCE: A sentence that shows the humans think the *dog* is the annoying one is, "_____."

3. FUN FIND: An *onomatopoeia* is a word that sounds like its meaning, such as *clucks*. Can you find two? A sentence containing two onomatopoeias is: "_____."

4. CONTEXT CLUES: What do you think *pathetic* means?

☐ wise ☐ ridiculous ☐ ticklish

5. S-T-R-E-T-C-H: Is a human narrating this story? Cite text to support your claims.

Nixing a Nickname

Gary did not like the nickname Kelvyn had given him: "Goofball Gary." Kelvyn was the only one in the entire school who called him that. Gary did not like it one bit. He **contemplated** giving Kelvyn a bad nickname as revenge, but decided not to. Two wrongs didn't make a right. Here's what Gary did instead. He talked calmly to Kelvyn to make him think about hurtful nicknames. Gary asked Kelvyn, "How would you feel if I called you 'Kooky Kelvyn'?"

"I would not like that," said Kelvyn.

"So now you can understand that I don't like being called 'Goofball Gary.'"

Kelvyn got the message. He never used the nickname again. Soon, Gary and Kelvyn even became friends.

KEY QUESTIONS

Cite text for all questions except #4.

1. CONFLICT: A sentence that shows this story's conflict is: "_____."

2. RESOLUTION: A sentence that shows the resolution is: "_____."

3. FUN FIND: According to the text, this is why Gary decided not to give Kelvyn a hurtful nickname: "_____."

4. CONTEXT CLUES: What do you think *contemplated* means?

☐ insulted ☐ agreed to
☐ thought about

5. S-T-R-E-T-C-H: What surprising thing happens at the very end of the story? Cite text to support your claim.

Samson Runs Off

Kwamie and his family were all set to watch the 4th of July fireworks. They settled on a blanket in the park. "They" was everyone—Kwamie, Kim, Mom, Dad, and Samson, their terrier. When the fireworks began thundering overhead, Samson got spooked and took off. Kwamie and his dad jumped up and ran after him. They raced through the city park. But Samson was a fast runner, and eventually they lost sight of him. Kwamie was heartbroken. He and his parents packed up their blanket and **trudged** home sadly. But as they neared their house, Kwamie couldn't believe his eyes. There on the front porch was Samson, waiting for them to return.

KEY QUESTIONS

Cite text for all questions except #4.

1. SETTING: A sentence that shows where the first part of the story is set is: "_____."

2. SETTING: What does Kwamie see when he gets home? According to the text, "_____."

3. FUN FIND: How does Kwamie feel when he loses sight of Samson? According to the text, "_____."

4. CONTEXT CLUES: What do you think *trudged* means?

☐ skipped ☐ walked slowly ☐ drove

5. S-T-R-E-T-C-H: Did Samson enjoy the fireworks? Cite text to support your claim.

Rained Out

All week Sam had been looking forward to Saturday. He and his parents had tickets to a baseball game. Sam loved baseball, but he had never been to a game before. When he woke up on Saturday, he noticed that the sky was very dark. Soon the rain started falling. And it fell and it fell, harder and harder. The ballgame was canceled. Sam was crushed. His big day was going to be ruined! But his dad had an **alternate** plan. A new movie with Sam's favorite superhero was opening that very day. So they all put on their raincoats and headed out to the theater. Sam had a great time.

KEY QUESTIONS

Cite text for all questions except #4.

1. CONFLICT: A sentence that shows the story's conflict is, "_____."

2. RESOLUTION: A sentence that shows the story's resolution is, "_____."

3. FUN FIND: What does Sam see when he wakes up on Saturday? According to the text, "_____."

4. CONTEXT CLUES: What do you think *alternate* means?

☐ another ☐ popcorn
☐ umbrella

5. S-T-R-E-T-C-H: Does Sam end up enjoying the new plan? Cite text to support your claim.

Finders Keepers?

Manuel sat on a sidewalk bench watching people go by. A man passed by and accidentally dropped some money. Manuel jumped up and grabbed it. It was a twenty-dollar bill! "Oh, boy," he said to himself. "Just think of all the things I could do with twenty dollars!" He watched the man walking away, completely **unaware** that he'd dropped his money. Manuel thought how bad he would feel if he'd lost all that money. So he ran after the man and gave him back the twenty dollars. A few minutes later, the man returned. He had a giant ice cream cone for Manuel, along with plenty of thanks.

KEY QUESTIONS

Cite text for all questions except #4.

1. CHARACTER: A sentence that shows Manuel is a kind person is: "_____."

2. CHARACTER: A sentence that shows that the man feels grateful is: "_____."

3. FUN FIND: What does Manuel do when the man drops the money? The author says, "_____."

4. CONTEXT CLUES: What do you think *unaware* means?

☐ not liking ☐ not knowing
☐ not caring

5. S-T-R-E-T-C-H: Would Manuel agree with the rhyme, "Finders keepers, losers weepers"? Cite text to support your claim.

Moat Party

Ann was a twelve-year-old princess. She lived in a big, stone castle in a land called Calazee. It was long, long ago in the Middle Ages. But Ann felt like she hadn't had any fun since forever. Being a young princess involved so many duties. She had to attend ceremonies and do lots of bowing and waving. So one day, she decided to throw a party. As it happened, her castle was surrounded by a moat filled with water. It was the perfect spot because the water was warm and there weren't any alligators. All the kids in the kingdom had a great time splashing around. From then on, Princess Ann held an **annual** moat party. It was the hit of the kingdom!

KEY QUESTIONS

Cite text for all questions except #4.

1. SETTING: A sentence that tells where this story takes place is, "_____."

2. SETTING: A sentence that tells when this story takes place is, "_____."

3. FUN FIND: According to the text, these were Ann's duties: "_____."

4. CONTEXT CLUES: What do you think *annual* means?

☐ fun ☐ by invitation only
☐ yearly

5. S-T-R-E-T-C-H: Was Princess Ann's party a success? Cite text to support your claim.

TEXT EVIDENCE: LITERARY

The Perfect Pet

Lina and Carlos were siblings. They usually got along, but right now they were having a serious disagreement. They could not decide what kind of dog to get. Lina wanted a poodle. "Poodles are smart, and they don't shed," she said. But Carlos wanted a golden retriever. "They play fetch, and they're loyal and sweet." Finally, their mom suggested a **compromise**. "How about a golden doodle?" Lina and Carlos looked at her. "Huh?" Their mom explained that a golden doodle was a cross between a golden retriever and a poodle. "You both win!" she said. So they got a golden doodle, and they were both thrilled.

KEY QUESTIONS

Cite text for all questions except #4.

1. CONFLICT: A sentence that shows the conflict in this story is: "_____."

2. RESOLUTION: A sentence that shows how this conflict is resolved is: "_____."

3. FUN FIND: What two dogs is a golden doodle a cross between? According to the story, "_____."

4. CONTEXT CLUES: What do you think *compromise* means?

☐ problem ☐ deal ☐ promise

5. S-T-R-E-T-C-H: Does this story have a happy or sad ending? Cite text to support your claim.

TEXT EVIDENCE: LITERARY

Ruler of the Universe

"I am the ruler of the WHOLE universe," shouted a silver-faced space alien with pointy ears and a long cape. "The Earthlings have risen up against me. I will make them pay for the rest of their silly little lives!" Then he cackled cruelly.

"And cut," said the movie director. "Great work today, Dave."

Dave had done a very fine job of acting. He walked over and got an apple juice. He was still wearing his silver makeup and long cape. He smiled and talked **amiably** with the other actors. Then his cellphone rang. It was his daughter. Dave answered his phone in a friendly voice. "Hi sweetie," he said. "How was your day at school?"

KEY QUESTIONS

Cite text for all questions except #4.

1. INFERENCE: This sentence tells you that the alien is make-believe: "_____."

2. INFERENCE: This sentence tells you that Dave is different from the cruel space alien that he plays: "_____."

3. FUN FIND: Here's the first thing Dave did after he was done filming for the day: "_____."

4. CONTEXT CLUES: What do you think *amiably* means?

☐ in a friendly way
☐ in a nasty way
☐ in a funny way

5. S-T-R-E-T-C-H: Is Dave a good or bad actor? Cite text to support your claim.

My Friend Inez

Inez was the most popular kid at our school. Everyone liked her. She was kind and never said mean things about people. Sometimes popular kids thought they were **superior** to everyone else, but Inez was nice to everyone. One day not long ago, Inez saw a second grader being teased by some older kids. Inez stepped in and told the bullies to stop. And they did—instantly. They felt bad about their mean behavior and stopped picking on others. They even apologized. Inez did awesome stuff like that all the time. She didn't have to try hard to be nice, she just was.

KEY QUESTIONS

Cite text for all questions except #4.

1. CHARACTER: A sentence that describes Inez's personality is, "_____."

2. CHARACTER: How is Inez unlike some popular kids? According to the story, "_____."

3. FUN FIND: How do the bullies change because of Inez? The author says, "_____."

4. CONTEXT CLUES: What do you think *superior* means?

☐ different ☐ better ☐ popular

5. S-T-R-E-T-C-H: Would you like to have a friend like Inez? Why? Cite text to support your claim.

Hangry Jack

It was the fifth day of their family vacation. Jack was out of sorts. Riding in the car had grown irritating. He stared out the window. Even seeing mountains and deer wasn't fun anymore. *A mountain is just a big, dumb rock*, he thought. *A deer is just a boring brown mammal with antlers. Big deal!* Jack's mother saw him **grimace**. "You seem hangry," she said, handing him a granola bar.

Hungry plus *angry* = *hangry*. That's sure how Jack felt. He ate the granola bar and stared out the window. Suddenly, the whole world just seemed so much better and Jack felt awesome. "Look over there at the bottom of that incredible mountain," he said. "There's a gorgeous deer!" *Yup, happy Jack was back.*

KEY QUESTIONS

Cite text for all questions except #4.

1. TONE: This story has an angry tone. A sentence that shows this angry tone is: "_____."

2. TONE: Another sentence that shows this angry tone is: "_____."

3. FUN FIND: What does "hangry" mean? According to the story: "_____."

4. CONTEXT CLUES: What do you think *grimace* means?

☐ a very unhappy look
☐ a very joyful look
☐ a very goofy look

5. S-T-R-E-T-C-H: How does eating the granola bar help Jack? Cite text to support your claim.

Two Weeks at Camp

When Mitchell arrived at summer camp, his stomach was tied in knots. The camp was in the Ozark Mountains, 150 miles from home. This was the first time he'd been so far away from his parents. Both his mom and dad told him about all the fun they had at summer camp when they were kids. But Mitchell wasn't convinced. He was quiet and shy. And he was also secretly **dreading** camp. Soon he met two of his cabinmates. They were friendly and outgoing. They had been to camp before, and they told Mitchell they would be his buddies. Suddenly Mitchell thought camp might not be so bad after all.

KEY QUESTIONS

Cite text for all questions except #4.

1. CHARACTER: A sentence that describes Mitchell's personality is, "_____."

2. CHARACTER: A sentence that describes Mitchell's cabinmates is, "_____."

3. FUN FIND: This sentence tells where the story is set "_____."

4. CONTEXT CLUES: What do you think *dreading* means?

☐ fearing ☐ remembering ☐ hoping

5. S-T-R-E-T-C-H: When Mitchell arrives at camp is he thrilled or scared? Cite text to support your claim.

Gabby, the Goalie

Gabby had never played goalie before. She had butterflies in her stomach. Tam, the other team's star player, had the soccer ball. Tam ran towards Gabby, kicking the ball ahead of her. Little beads of sweat formed on Gabby's forehead. Closer and closer came Tam until she was only a few feet away. Gabby's legs went kind of wobbly. Tam kicked the ball. It sailed through the air. Gabby grabbed it and kept it from going into the goal. Just like that, Gabby became **composed** and confident. Her team won 2-0, and Gabby, the goalie, was the star.

KEY QUESTIONS

Cite text for all questions except #4.

1. TONE: This story has a nervous tone. A sentence that shows this nervous tone is: "_____."

2. TONE: Another sentence that show this nervous tone is: "_____."

3. FUN FIND: A saying that compares nervousness to an insect is: "_____."

4. CONTEXT CLUES: What do you think *composed* means?

☐ athletic ☐ calm ☐ musical

5. S-T-R-E-T-C-H: Does Gabby overcome her nervousness at the end of the story? Cite text to support your claim.

Flying High

Martine swooped and soared. She flew high in the sky. Down below she saw her house. Her mom stood out front and waved to Martine. Martine flew over her school and saw her friends out at recess. She watched them play games and run around. But still she kept flying! She had always wanted to fly. It was the best feeling ever. A moment later she heard her mother **uttering** her name softly. "Martine, Martine. It's time to wake up, honey."

Martine opened her eyes and saw her mom's face, and the light blue walls of her room. It was Monday morning, time to get up and go to school.

KEY QUESTIONS

Cite text for all questions except #4.

1. SETTING: At the end of the story, you learn where the story really takes place. A sentence that shows this is, "_____."

2. SETTING: At the end of the story, a sentence that shows when the story takes place is: "_____."

3. FUN FIND: A sentence that shows what Martine sees while she's flying is, "_____."

4. CONTEXT CLUES: What do you think *uttering* means?

☐ believing ☐ saying ☐ remembering

5. S-T-R-E-T-C-H: Does Martine like flying or is she scared? Cite text to support your claim.

Which Watch?

Dexter wanted a wristwatch for his birthday. His grandmother took him shopping so he could pick out the perfect one. He narrowed it down to two—one analog and one digital. Both watches were waterproof. Both had faces that lit up in the dark. The digital watch **displayed** the time in numbers, but the analog watch used hands to show the time. The analog watch showed the seconds, but the digital watch showed only the hours and minutes. Dexter ended up choosing the analog watch because it had a cool camouflage band. He strapped it on and looked at his wrist. "It's 1:15 and forty seconds. Time for lunch!"

KEY QUESTIONS

Cite text for all questions except #4.

1. COMPARE: How are the two watches similar? The story says, "_____."

2. CONTRAST: How are the two watches different? The story says, "_____."

3. FUN FIND: Why does Dexter choose the analog watch? According to the story, "_____."

4. CONTEXT CLUES: What do you think *displayed* means?

☐ showed ☐ counted ☐ bought

5. S-T-R-E-T-C-H: Does Dexter's dad take him watch shopping? Cite text to support your claim.

Slurp! Smack!

Bart loved spaghetti more than anything! Someone would place a bowl of spaghetti in front of Bart. Bart would slurp up the noodles, one by one. *Slurp!* A single noodle slid into his mouth. *Smack!* Bart made this sound as it disappeared. But then Bart visited his friend Mike for dinner. To his great **chagrin**, Mike's Mom served spaghetti. *Egads!* How could Bart possibly eat it in an un-silly way? Then, Mike's father used his fork to lift a single noodle to his lips. *Slurp! Smack!* Mike's mother did the same. *Slurp! Smack!* Mike and Bart joined in, and soon everyone slurped and smacked with glee. The meal tasted grand and was super silly—just the way Bart liked it.

KEY QUESTIONS

Cite text for all questions except #4.

1. CAUSE: A sentence that states the cause is: "_____."

2. EFFECT: A sentence that states the effect is: "_____."

3. FUN FIND: What is Bart's favorite food? According to the story, "_____."

4. CONTEXT CLUES: What do you think *chagrin* means?

☐ amusement ☐ anger
☐ nervous embarrassment

5. S-T-R-E-T-C-H: Did Bart end up enjoying his meal? Cite text to support your claim.

Hey, That Dog Looks Just Like Me!

Charlie was a three-month-old pup that had never seen a mirror before. "Someone new to play with!" he thought when he saw his reflection. The other puppy was the same size as Charlie. It was even the same breed. Charlie and the dog were like two peas in a pod. "Hey," Charlie barked, "let's go play!" The puppy didn't answer. It just stood there, **gazing** back at him. Charlie felt sad that the dog didn't want to play. The girl who lived in the house came home and said, "Charlie! Are you barking at your reflection? Let's go play fetch." Charlie followed the girl. She was *much* more fun than that silly dog.

KEY QUESTIONS

Cite text for all questions except #4.

1. CHARACTER: A sentence that shows Charlie is young is: "_____."

2. CHARACTER: A sentence that shows how Charlie feels when the other dog doesn't want to play is: "_____."

3. FUN FIND: A simile compares two unlike things using the word *like* or *as*. *Roar like a lion* is a simile. A sentence that contains a simile is: "_____."

4. CONTEXT CLUES: What do you think *gazing* means?

☐ barking ☐ looking ☐ smiling

5. S-T-R-E-T-C-H: Who does Charlie like to play with more than the pup in the mirror? Cite text to support your claim.

Fixing a Fight

Merry had sent a bunch of texts, but Sophie had not responded. Sophie tried to give an explanation. She'd been so busy with homework that she hadn't even looked at her phone. Now Merry was mad and stormed off in a huff.

So Sophie came up with an idea to **remedy** the problem. She decided to send Merry a special text to show her how much she cared. It read: "BBFFAA = Best-Best Friends Forever And Always."

Almost immediately, a text came back from Merry: "Awww. I feel the same way. Hugs."

KEY QUESTIONS

Cite text for all questions except #4.

1. CONFLICT: A sentence that shows this story's conflict is: "_____."

2. RESOLUTION: A sentence that shows the resolution is: "_____."

3. FUN FIND: Why doesn't Sophie respond to Merry's text? According to the story, "_____."

4. CONTEXT CLUES: What do you think *remedy* means?

☐ forget ☐ increase ☐ fix

5. S-T-R-E-T-C-H: What does BBFFAA stand for? Cite text to support your claim.

Kamal's Choice

Kamal loved the piano. He dreamed of playing beautiful, **majestic** music—music like famous pianists played. But he hated to practice! "Practice is so boring!" he said. When his teacher told Kamal he wasn't ready to play in the big recital, Kamal didn't listen, and he played anyway. It did not go well. He made lots of mistakes. "You could be a very good pianist," his teacher said. "But only if you work hard. The choice is yours." Now Kamal understood that he had to choose to work if he wanted to be good at something. He practiced every day over the next six months. And guess what? At the next recital, Kamal got a standing ovation!

KEY QUESTIONS

Cite text for all questions except #4.

1. THEME: A sentence that shows the theme of the story is: "_____."

2. THEME: A sentence that shows Kamal's new attitude is: "_____."

3. FUN FIND: What happens at the very end of the story? According to the text, "_____."

4. CONTEXT CLUES: What do you think *majestic* means?

☐ ugly ☐ grand ☐ funny

5. S-T-R-E-T-C-H: Why is *Kamal's Choice* a good title for this story? Cite text to support your claim.

Bedtime for Fireflies

It was 7:00 A.M., and the sun shone brightly. The family of fireflies needed to go to bed. Mama and Papa Firefly kissed their kids and tucked them in. The whole bug family was **snug**. The fireflies hung out on the cool, shady underside of a leaf. But the firefly kids were too excited to sleep. They kept fluttering their wings and lighting up their tails.

"Stop flashing your lights and go to sleep," said Mama Firefly.

"Settle down," said Papa Firefly. "You're going to keep everyone up all day."

KEY QUESTIONS

Cite text for all questions except #4.

1. SETTING: A sentence that tells where this story takes place is, "_____."

2. SETTING: A sentence that tells when this story takes place is, "_____."

3. FUN FIND: According to the story, instead of going to sleep, the firefly kids did this: "_____."

4. CONTEXT CLUES: What do you think *snug* means?

☐ tired and tense
☐ cozy and comfortable
☐ awake and alert

5. S-T-R-E-T-C-H: Did the firefly kids fall right to sleep? Cite text to support your claim.

Couch Calm

Deon had the couch all to himself. His little brother was playing in the yard. His little sister was in her room. Deon made a big bowl of popcorn. It was so nice not to have anybody grabbing handfuls. He put on his favorite TV show. It was so calm with nobody fighting over the remote. Deon took off his shoes, stretched out on the couch, and relaxed. He enjoyed about half an hour of pure **bliss**. Then, his little brother and sister rushed into the room at exactly the same time. His brother snatched a handful of popcorn. His sister grabbed the remote. *Oh well*, thought Deon, *it was nice while it lasted.*

KEY QUESTIONS

Cite text for all questions except #4.

1. TONE: This story has a mostly peaceful tone. A sentence that shows this peaceful tone is: "_____."

2. TONE: Another sentence that shows the peaceful tone is: "_____."

3. FUN FIND: According to the text, this was Deon's snack: "_____."

4. CONTEXT CLUES: What do you think *bliss* means?

☐ raging anger   ☐ desperate sadness
☐ peaceful joy

5. S-T-R-E-T-C-H: Will Deon's couch calm continue? Cite text to support your claim.

The Prankster

Gus was a mischievous guy. He always played pranks on people. Gus popped out of a clothes hamper, making his mother scream. He put a pickle in his little brother's shoe. But then he dreamed up a real doozy. One evening, he switched the **contents** of the milk and orange juice cartons. He couldn't wait to see what happened. Maybe his dad would pour juice in his coffee. Only problem: by the next morning, Gus forgot what he'd done. At breakfast, he tried to pour milk onto his cereal and added orange juice instead. *Yuck!* The whole family laughed. Gus had pranked himself!

KEY QUESTIONS

Cite text for all questions except #4.

1. CHARACTER: A sentence that describes Gus's personality is: "_____."

2. CHARACTER: Another sentence that describes his personality is: "_____."

3. FUN FIND: This sentence tells about the prank Gus played on his brother: "_____."

4. CONTEXT CLUES: What do you think *contents* means?

☐ things you eat
☐ things you drink
☐ what's contained in something

5. S-T-R-E-T-C-H: Who does Gus prank at the end of the story? Cite text to support your claim.

A Leaf's Life

Annette hung on to the tree for dear life. She had enjoyed her green **hue** all spring and summer. As the weather changed, Annette turned a lovely, bright red. She had been the brightest on her tree branch. But now it was October, and she was a dull, crispy brown. All it would take was one big gust of wind to send her spiraling down to the ground. She was quite nervous about falling, but most of her pals had already made the journey. What would it be like to spin through the air? For now, she would just enjoy the sunshine and the sound of a nearby bird singing.

KEY QUESTIONS

Cite text for all questions except #4.

1. SETTING: A sentence that shows where this story is set is: "_____."

2. TIME: A sentence that shows what season the story takes place in is: "_____."

3. FUN FIND: What was the first color Annette turned as the weather changed? According to the story, "_____."

4. CONTEXT CLUES: What do you think *hue* means?

☐ friend ☐ sound ☐ color

5. S-T-R-E-T-C-H: Is Annette worried about falling from the tree? Cite text to support your claim.

Enjoying a Cloud Show

Tanya sat on a country hillside. It was a warm summer afternoon. The sky above was blue and filled with puffy, white clouds. Tanya studied a cloud. It was shaped almost exactly like Australia. The cloud's shape shifted, and soon it looked like a pair of glasses. Tanya looked at another cloud. It **resembled** a table with a vase of flowers. Soon this cloud changed, too. Last, it looked like a llama balancing a beach ball on its nose. What a way to spend an afternoon! While simply lying on a hillside, Tanya's imagination showed her all kinds of strange and wonderful things.

KEY QUESTIONS

Cite text for all questions except #4.

1. SETTING: A sentence that tells where this story takes place is, "_____."

2. SETTING: A sentence that tells when this story takes place is, "_____."

3. FUN FIND: What continent did the cloud look like? According to the story, "_____."

4. CONTEXT CLUES: What do you think *resembled* means?

☐ puffy   ☐ floated by
☐ looked like

5. S-T-R-E-T-C-H: Is the last cloud shape that Tanya sees a bear riding a bike? Cite text to support your claim.

The Twin Twins

Ava and Abby were identical twin sisters. They looked alike, with blue eyes and blond hair. Both had names that started with the same letter. They even both loved music. But Ava and Abby played different instruments. Ava played the guitar, while Abby played the drums. They met another set of twins who played the piano and bass. Together, the four of them were the perfect **combination** to form a band. And guess what they called their band? The Twin Twins!

KEY QUESTIONS

Cite text for all questions except #4.

1. COMPARE: A sentence that shows how Ava and Abby are alike is: "_____."

2. CONTRAST: A sentence that shows how the twins are different is: "_____."

3. FUN FIND: This sentence tells what instruments the other band members played: "_____."

4. CONTEXT CLUES: What do you think *combination* means?

☐ the mixing of different parts
☐ rock stars   ☐ separate

5. S-T-R-E-T-C-H: Did the kids name their band *The Fab Foursome*? Cite text to support your claim.

TEXT EVIDENCE: INFORMATIONAL

Cat-egories (Card 1)
1. A sentence that includes the main idea is: "There are many kinds of house cats."
2. A sentence with a detail is: "Around 50 different breeds exist." (Other answers possible.)
3. According to the text, "The Ocicat has spots."
4. *Devoid* means "without."
5. No. The text says, "The LaPerm actually has curly fur, which looks like it has been styled at a salon."

Horrible Hilarious Hiccups! (Card 2)
1. According to the text, "Sometimes, the diaphragm contracts too quickly."
2. According to the passage, "That causes you to hiccup over and over."
3. The text states, "The longest case of hiccups ever recorded was 68 years!"
4. *Contracts* means "tightens."
5. Yes. According to the text, "Normally hiccups last for only a few minutes."

Snow and Salt (Card 3)
1. This sentence shows a similarity between snow and salt: "Both are white and both consist of crystals." (Other answers possible.)
2. This sentence shows a difference between snow and salt: "They sure don't taste the same though." (Other answers possible.)
3. This sentence describes the shape of a salt crystal: "If you study an individual salt crystal, you'll see it's shaped like a tiny cube."
4. *Individual* means "single."
5. No. The text states, "Looking at a snowflake under a microscope, you can see little ice crystals in the shape of a star."

The Stinkiest Animals on Earth! (Card 4)
1. A sentence that describes how zorillas look is: "They have flat faces, small ears, and long, bushy tails." (Other answers possible.)
2. A sentence that describes how zorillas communicate is: "They communicate with growls and high-pitched screams." (Other answers possible.)
3. The author states, "Zorillas are also known as striped polecats."
4. *Foul-smelling* means "bad-smelling."
5. No. According to the text, "Like skunks, zorillas spray a foul-smelling scent to keep predators away." (Other answers possible.)

Should Kids Have Chores? (Card 5)
1. This sentence argues in favor of chores for kids: "They say chores help kids develop responsibility and self-reliance." (Other answers possible.)
2. This sentence argues against chores for kids: "They argue that kids should be focused on their homework and other activities that will bring them success." (Other answers possible.)
3. No. According to the text, "When it comes to this issue, different people have very different ideas."
4. *Self-reliance* means "independence."
5. The text states, "They say chores help kids develop responsibility and self-reliance." I agree. That is why I believe kids should have chores. (Other answers possible.)

Dandy Dandelions (Card 6)
1. A fact in the text is: "The dandelion is a very common plant with yellow flowers." (Other answers possible.)
2. An opinion in the text is: "Dandelions are beautiful." (Other answers possible.)
3. A sentence that compares seeds to something else is: "If you blow on them, the seeds float through the air like tiny parachutes."
4. *Nuisance* means "a bother."
5. The text says, "Dandelions are beautiful. They're also edible." I believe dandelions are a good plant for these two reasons. (Other answers possible.)

Pompeii (Card 7)
1. The first thing that happens is: "A famous volcano erupted nearly two thousand years ago."

2. Something that happens later in the text is: "The volcano's powerful eruption buried a whole city called Pompeii." (Other answers possible.)
3. I thought this detail was interesting: "Beneath the ash, they found a community frozen in time." (Other answers possible.)
4. *Preserved* means "kept as original."
5. The passage states, "Then, in the 1700s, archaeologists discovered the lost city of Pompeii." That means that it was discovered after the year 1600.

All About Deserts (Card 8)
1. A sentence that includes the main idea is: "A desert is a very common habitat."
2. A sentence with a detail is: "About one third of the Earth is covered in desert." (Other answers possible.)
3. A sentence that mentions three desert animals is: "Desert creatures include lizards, foxes, and penguins."
4. *Habitat* means "an animal home."
5. The writer states, "A desert is an area that usually gets less than 10 inches of rain in a year." I really dislike rain. For that reason, I would love to live in a desert. (Other answers possible.)

The Royal Dragon (Card 9)
1. Here is a sentence that tells how many people can eat at the Royal Dragon: "It has room for 5,000 diners."
2. Here is a sentence that tells what's considered lucky at the restaurant: "If a waiter glides down the zip line to serve your table, it is considered good luck."
3. A sentence that mentions chili peppers is: "The menu features spicy Thai food, such as squid with chili peppers."
4. *Interior* means "inside."
5. The passage says, "There is also a zip line that servers use to deliver some of the meals." That sounds fun, so I would love to be a server! (Other answers possible.)

Turning Green (Card 10)
1. According to the passage, "The salt and moisture in the air reacted with the copper."
2. According to the passage, "This reaction, a process called oxidation, turned the copper green."
3. The text states, "The giant statue is one of the United States' great symbols of freedom."

4. *Liberty* means "freedom."
5. No. The first sentence says, "Even if you've never been to its home in New York City, you've probably seen an image of the Statue of Liberty."

Reflexes (Card 11)
1. A sentence that states the cause is: "Something threatens to harm you."
2. A sentence that states the effect is: "Your reflexes kick in."
3. This sentence tells what happens if something bothers your nose: "If something irritates your nose, you will sneeze to get rid of it."
4. *Involuntarily* means "without thinking."
5. Reflexes are helpful. The text states, "The reason we have reflexes is for quick protection, without even having to think." (Other answers possible.)

Bugs for Breakfast? (Card 12)
1. A fact in the text is: "In fact, about 80 percent of the world's population regularly eats bugs." (Other answers possible.)
2. An opinion in the text is: "That sounds pretty gross!" (Other answers possible.)
3. I thought this fact was interesting: "Grasshoppers, they say, taste salty and spicy." (Other answers possible.)
4. *Plentiful* means "in large number."
5. Yes. The text states, "Bugs are all around us, and they provide a good source of protein." Those are two good reasons for people to eat bugs. (Other answers possible.)

Big Planet, Small Planet (Card 13)
1. In the text, a similarity between Mercury and Neptune is: "They both travel around the sun." (Other answers possible.)
2. In the text, a difference between the two planets is: "Mercury is the smallest planet in the solar system, while Neptune is quite large." (Other answers possible.)
3. This sentence tells how cold Neptune can get: "Its temperature can drop to more than 350 degrees below zero."
4. *Orbit* means "travel around."
5. No. The texts states, "During a day on Mercury, the temperature can reach 800 degrees." That is too hot for humans to survive! (Other answers possible.)

Every Four Years (Card 14)

1. According to the text, the thing that starts the process is: "First, about eighteen months before election day, Democratic and Republican candidates announce their plans to run for president."
2. According to the text, the last thing that happens is: "Finally, in November, Americans vote to decide who will be the next president."
3. The author says, "They're a bit like the playoffs in sports."
4. *Campaign* means "try to get people to vote for you."
5. No. According to the text, "Finally, in November, Americans vote to decide who will be the next president."

The Mighty Blue Whale (Card 15)

1. A sentence that includes the main idea is: "The blue whale is the largest creature on Earth."
2. A sentence with an important detail is: "Adults can grow to 100 feet long and weigh more than 200 tons." (Other answers possible.)
3. According to the text, "They can consume four tons of krill in a single day!"
4. *Emit* means "send out."
5. According to the text, "The blue whale is the largest creature on Earth." That is a good reason for them to be named "king of the ocean." (Other answers possible.).

Elisha Otis's Great Invention (Card 16)

1. The problem in the text is: "Tall buildings were troublesome because people would get exhausted walking up and down all the steps."
2. The solution in the text is: "Elisha Otis invented the modern elevator."
3. I thought this fact was extra interesting: "Otis's first elevators ran on steam power." (Other answers possible.)
4. *Crucial* means "very important."
5. The text says, "Elevators made it possible to build really tall buildings." The title is good because elevators are a great invention. (Other answers possible.)

The Voyage of the *Titanic* (Card 17)

1. The author states, "It stretched as long as three football fields and stood as tall as a 17-story building."

2. According to the text, "It was constructed of steel."
3. The text states, "*The Titanic* could carry 3,500 people."
4. *Perished* means "died."
5. The text states, "Its builders made use of the most advanced shipbuilding techniques of the time. For this reason, folks said the ship was 'unsinkable.' "

Is It a Meteor or a Meteorite? (Card 18)

1. According to the text, "Both are small bodies from outer space that enter Earth's atmosphere."
2. According to the text, "Unlike meteors, meteorites don't completely burn up."
3. The author states, "Between five and ten meteorites strike Earth each year."
4. *Strike* means "hit."
5. The text states, "Meteors leave a visible trail behind them." That trail probably makes them look like shooting stars even though they are not really stars. (Other answers possible.)

An Amazing Landing on the Hudson River (Card 19)

1. According to the text, "Some of the birds got trapped in the plane's engines, and the jet suddenly lost all power."
2. The author states, "He navigated the jet over to the Hudson River so he could land the plane on water."
3. According to the text, "Sullenberger stayed calm."
4. *Navigated* means "steered."
5. The text says, "He navigated the jet over to the Hudson River so he could land the plane on water." It also says, "All 155 people on board were safe." These facts show that Sullenberger was a hero. (Other answers possible.)

How Plants Make Food (Card 20)

1. The first step is, "A plant drinks water."
2. The second step is, "A plant's leaves absorb sunlight."
3. A sentence that tells who needs oxygen is, "People and animals do."
4. *Absorb* means "soak up."
5. The passage says: "Next, the plant mixes together water, sunlight, and a gas called carbon dioxide. This makes sugar, which is the plant's food."

The Best Pizza? (Card 21)

1. A sentence that tells how the two pizzas are similar is: "Both are round pies, with a bready crust." (Other answers possible.)
2. A sentence that tells how the two pizzas are different is: "But while New York-style pizza has a thin crust, the crust on Chicago-style pizza is thick." (Other answers possible.)
3. According to the text, "Most people agree that pizza is delicious."
4. *Diverge* means "divide."
5. The text says, "New York pizzas are flat, and you can eat them with your hands, but Chicago pizzas are deep-dish and you need a fork and knife." I like to eat with my hands so I think New York-style pizza is the best! (Other answers possible.)

Wide World of Rodents (Card 22)

1. A fact in the text is: "Rodents are a type of mammal." (Other answers possible.)
2. An opinion in the text is: "Now, that's one scary rodent!" (Other answers possible.)
3. Another interesting fact in the text is: "The biggest rodent is the capybara." (Other answers possible.)
4. *Atypical* means "unusual."
5. No. According to the text, "The biggest rodent in the capybara."

Life on Other Planets? (Card 23)

1. This sentence argues that life might exist elsewhere in the universe: "Other planets circling other stars could be suitable homes to living creatures." (Other answers possible.)
2. This sentence argues that life is only on Earth: "Every other place might have problems like being too hot, too cold, or too dry." (Other answers possible.)
3. This sentence states the debate topic: "Is there life elsewhere in the universe?"
4. *Unique* means "one of a kind."
5. The text states, "Because the universe is so vast, chances are good that somewhere out there life exists." I agree and believe life probably exists on other planets. (Other answer possible.)

The Famous Leaning Tower (Card 24)

1. The text states, "It was built on soil that was too soft to support it."
2. According to the text, "The tower is tilting."
3. The text says, "The Tower of Pisa is a very old tower in the city of Pisa, in Italy."

4. *Tourist attraction* means "place tourists visit."
5. No. The text states: "It's an extremely popular tourist attraction for an unusual reason."

Bats and Birds (Card 25)

1. In the text, a similarity between bats and birds is: "Bats and birds are warm-blooded." (Other answers possible.)
2. In the text, a difference between the two is: "Bats have fur, while birds have feathers." (Other answers possible.)
3. This sentence list three animals bats are related to: "That's right, bats are part of the same group of animals that includes mice, elephants, and humans."
4. *Generate* means "make."
5. No. The text says, "Bats have fur, while birds have feathers."

Copernicus, Ahead of His Time (Card 26)

1. A fact in the text is: "All the planets, including Earth, orbit this star." (Other answers possible.)
2. An opinion in the text is: "I think that idea is pretty funny." (Other answers possible.)
3. The author states, "At the time, people didn't believe Copernicus."
4. *Opposed* means "disagreed with."
5. According to the text, "He wrote a book explaining that Earth actually rotated around the sun." Back then, people did not know this fact. For that reason, Copernicus was ahead of his time. (Other answers possible.)

Ouch! Brain Freeze (Card 27)

1. According to the text, "When a very cold substance hits the roof of your mouth, blood flow increases."
2. The text says, "The increased blood flow triggers pain in the head."
3. The author states, "Some call it *ice-cream headache*."
4. *Piercing* means "sharp. "
5. No. The text says: "Not everyone experiences brain freeze when they eat something cold."

What a Place! (Card 28)

1. A sentence that describes the location of Santorini is: "It is a Greek island in the Mediterranean Sea."

2. A sentence that describes the beaches of Santorini is: "Some sand is black or red." (Other answers possible.)
3. A sentence that mentions an animal is: "You can get to the town by riding a donkey up a steep path."
4. *Spectacular* means "dramatically beautiful."
5. The text says, "Some sand is black or red." It also says, "Nothing compares to a spectacular Santorini sunset." For these reasons, I would love to go to there! (Other answers possible.)

Self-Driving Cars (Card 29)
1. This sentence gives an advantage of self-driving cars: "Maybe kids could even travel by themselves in a self-driving car." (Other answers possible.)
2. This sentence gives a disadvantage of self-driving cars: "Sometimes computers crash and that could cause the car to crash." (Other answers possible.)
3. According to the text, "Companies such as Google are busy experimenting with cars that use computers to drive themselves."
4. *Overreact* means "respond too strongly."
5. The passage says, "While the car drove itself, people could read or play video games." I love doing both things, so I would love a self-driving car. (Other answers possible.)

Hey, You! Get Lost! (Card 30)
1. A sentence that tells the main idea is: "When it comes to dodging enemies, animals have a variety of strategies to say, 'Keep away!'"
2. According to the passage, "The tiny bombardier beetle keeps attackers away by spraying a super-hot liquid from its rear." (Other answers possible.)
3. A sentence that includes a simile is: "Its body appears as dead as a doornail."
4. *Inflates* means "blows up."
5. The passage says: "The tiny bombardier beetle keeps attackers away by spraying a super-hot liquid from its rear." That sounds gross, so I would not like one for a pet.

LOUD SOUNDS!!!!! (Card 31)
1. A sentence that states the cause is: "Sounds can be loud or even ear-splitting."
2. A sentence that states the effect is: "This can hurt your ears."

3. According to the text: "A loud rock concert can reach 120 decibels."
4. *Ear-splitting* means "very loud."
5. The author states, "Earplugs are a must—don't forget them!"

Telling Sea Lions From Seals (Card 32)
1. A sentence that tells how seals and sea lions are similar is: "They both have big, blubbery bodies." (Other answers possible.)
2. A sentence that tells how seals and sea lions are different is: "One difference is that sea lions can walk on land, but seals can't." (Other answers possible.)
3. A sentence containing an opinion is: "Seals and sea lions are two of the most lovable creatures in the ocean."
4. *Wriggling* means "wiggling."
5. No. The passage says, "Both have big dark eyes, long whiskers, and two sets of flippers."

Haggis (Card 33)
1. Here's a fact in the text: "Burns Night is a celebration of a famous Scottish poet named Robert Burns." (Other answers possible.)
2. Here's an opinion in the text: "Haggis does not sound tasty." (Other answers possible.)
3. The text says, "It's a kind of pudding made from parts of a sheep's heart, liver, and lungs."
4. *Recite* means "say aloud from memory."
5. The author states: "It's a kind of pudding made from parts of a sheep's heart, liver, and lungs." That makes me NOT want to eat it. (Other answers possible.)

The Making of Central Park (Card 34)
1. The problem in the text is: "New York City didn't have many open spaces where people could go to relax."
2. The solution in the text is: "Central Park was created."
3. According to the text, "The lake was perfect for row boating in summer and ice skating in winter."
4. *Oasis* means "calm spot."
5. The text says: "Thousands of trees were planted. Paths were laid out for people to walk on." Those things are very calming in the middle of a busy city. (Other answers possible.)

Spectacular Fireflies (Card 35)

1. A fact in the text is: "Fireflies are actually a kind of beetle." (Other answers possible.)
2. An opinion in the text is: "Fireflies are fabulous insects!" (Other answers possible.)
3. This detail in the text is very interesting to me: "Many people have never seen a firefly because they live only in certain parts of the country." (Other answers possible.)
4. *Brief* means "short."
5. The text says, "Fireflies are actually a kind of beetle." For that reason, I would call them "blinking beetles." (Answers will vary.)

School, Near and Far (Card 36)

1. A sentence that tells how school in Japan is similar to school here is: "They have art and music and sometimes go on field trips." (Other answers possible.)
2. A sentence that tells how school in Japan is different is: "In the U.S., kids attend school for about 160 days, but Japanese kids go for about 240." (Other answers possible.)
3. According to the text, "They even wear special indoor shoes to keep things tidy!"
4. *Attend* means "go to."
5. The author states: "In the U.S., kids attend school for about 160 days, but Japanese kids go for about 240." I love school! For that reason, I would like to go to school in Japan. (Other answers possible.)

A Very Long Bridge (Card 37)

1. This sentence tells the name of the bridge: "It is called the Danyang-Kunshan Grand Bridge."
2. This sentence gives its length: "The bridge is 102 miles long."
3. This sentence tells what kind of vehicle uses the bridge: "It is for high-speed trains."
4. *Spans* means "crosses."
5. No. According to the text, "Such land is perfect for growing rice so there are many rice farms here."

Parachuting Beavers (Card 38)

1. According to the author, the problem is: "There were too many beavers living near people."
2. According to the author, the solution is: "A plan was hatched to move the beavers to a better place."
3. This sentence describes the special boxes: "The boxes had airholes and parachutes attached."
4. *Cargo* means "items carried in a vehicle."
5. No. The text states, "Down floated the beavers to their new homes, deep in the woods and far away from people."

Dry, Dry, Droughts (Card 39)

1. A sentence that states the cause is: "Sometimes no rain falls for many weeks."
2. A sentence that states the effect is: "A drought sets in."
3. According to the text, "Plants may shrivel up or even die."
4. *Scarce* means "rare."
5. Here is one way: "People can also take showers rather than baths." (Other answers possible.)

Dogs: Paws Up or Paws Down? (Card 40)

1. This sentence states an advantage of dogs: "They are smart animals and can learn tricks." (Other answers possible.)
2. This sentence states a disadvantage of dogs: "Dogs can be messy." (Other answers possible.)
3. This sentence lists some pets besides dogs: "Consider a cat, bird, fish, hamster, or iguana."
4. *Downsides* means "disadvantages."
5. The text states, "Dogs enjoy spending time with people. They are smart animals and can learn tricks." These are two reasons I'd like a dog for a pet! (Other answers possible.)

From Oswald to Elsa (Card 41)

1. Here's a fact in the text: "Oswald was Walt Disney's first hit cartoon in 1927." (Other answers possible.)
2. Here's an opinion in the text: "I think *Frozen* is the best Disney movie ever!" (Other answers possible.)
3. Another opinion in the text is, "Elsa is an amazing character." (Other answers possible.)
4. *Rendered* means "drawn."
5. No. The author states: "I think *Frozen* is the best Disney movie ever!"

The Remarkable Rosa Parks (Card 42)

1. The sentence containing the main idea is, "Rosa Parks was an ordinary woman who ended up changing history."
2. According to the text, "One day Parks, an African American, refused to give up her bus seat to a white man."
3. According to the text, "The bus companies lost a lot of money, and soon the segregation laws were changed."
4. *Injustice* means "unfairness."
5. The text says, "Rosa Parks was an ordinary woman who ended up changing history." That is quite remarkable, so the title fits. (Other answers possible.)

Standing Tall When the Ground Shakes (Card 43)

1. The problem in the text is: "Big earthquakes, however, can do a lot of damage."
2. The solution in the text is: "Engineers developed a process called 'seismic retrofitting.'"
3. One detail in the text I found interesting is: "Most earthquakes are so small people can't even feel them." (Other answers possible.)
4. *Withstand* means "handle."
5. No. The text states, "Engineers developed a process called 'seismic retrofitting.'"

How to Make an Ice Cream Sundae— Any Day! (Card 44)

1. The author states, "First, you get a bowl to hold the sundae."
2. The author states, "Next, you scoop in your favorite flavor of ice cream."
3. A sentence that contains a simile is, "It's as easy as pie!"
4. *Drizzle* means "pour lightly."
5. No, the author writes: "The very last step is eating your sundae."

The Phases of the Moon (Card 45)

1. According to the text, "The reason the moon always looks different is because its position is always changing."
2. According to the text, "It's the different positions in the moon's orbit that change its appearance here on Earth."
3. The text says, "Some nights you look up at the moon and see a big round ball."
4. *Appearance* means "how something looks."
5. Yes. The author says, "And sometimes you can't see the moon at all."

Narwhals: Unicorns of the Sea (Card 46)

1. A sentence that tells how much fully grown narwhals weigh is: "Fully grown narwhals can reach 3,000 pounds."
2. A sentence that tells the length of the narwhal's horn is: "This horn is spiraled and can be up to ten feet long."
3. The author states, "But unicorns are mythical, which means they don't really exist."
4. *Protruding* means "sticking out"
5. The text says, "Narwhals have a long horn protruding from their head." That is why they are called sea unicorns. (Other answers possible.)

Aloha, Hawaii! (Card 47)

1. A sentence that includes the main idea in this text is: "Hawaii is an amazing place."
2. A sentence with a detail is: "The state is a group of 132 islands." (Other answers possible.)
3. This sentence contains alliteration: "But Hawaii isn't a landlocked state like Iowa, Illinois, or Indiana."
4. *Consist* means "to be made of."
5. No. The text states: "It's about halfway between California and Japan."

Should We Raise the Driving Age to 18? (Card 48)

1. A sentence that argues in favor of raising the driving age is: "Younger teens are more likely to be texting when they should be watching the road, they say." (Other answers possible.)
2. A sentence that argues against raising the driving age is: "Practice and experience are what really count." (Other answers possible.)
3. A sentence that contains a hyperbole is: "The important thing is making sure 16-year-olds have a gazillion hours of practice before they get their license."
4. *Appropriate* means "right."
5. The author states, "Younger teens are more likely to be texting when they should be watching the road, they say." For that reason, I think the driving age should be raised to 18. (Other answers possible.)

Umbrellas Are Also for Fellas (Card 49)

1. The problem in the text is: "In a rainstorm, you can easily get extremely wet."
2. The solution in the text is: "The umbrella was created to help a person stay dry."
3. Where was the umbrella invented? According to the text: "It was invented in the country of China."
4. *Merchant* is a "business person."
5. The text says, "At first, however, umbrellas were only used by women. Then, an Englishman named Jonas Hanway started using an umbrella in the 1700s." When you learn these facts, the title seems perfect. (Other answers possible.)

Horses, Of Course! (Card 50)

1. A sentence that tells when baby horses are born is: "Foals are usually born at night."
2. A sentence that tells how much a horse can weigh is: "Some stallions weigh 700 pounds or more."
3. A cowboy word at the very end of the passage is: "*Yeehaw!*"
4. *Herbivores* means plant eaters.
5. No. The passage says: "Horses don't eat any meat, which makes them herbivores."

TEXT EVIDENCE: LITERARY

Rain Forest Fashion (Card 51)

1. A sentence that tells where this story takes place is, "Her family was on a visit to the Amazon rain forest."
2. A sentence that tells when this story takes place is, "It was Cindy's summer vacation."
3. According to the story, this is what Cindy did at the shop: "Cindy picked out the most brightly colored T-shirt in the store."
4. *Gobsmacked* means "amazed."
5. No. The text states: "Cindy wore jeans and a white T-shirt."

Trudy Spills the Beans (Card 52)

1. The sentence that shows Mom knows about the secret is: "As they were leaving, Mom told everyone, 'Bring sweaters because it might be cold up in the balloon.'"
2. The sentence that shows everyone knows it was Trudy who told Mom is: "Everyone looked at Trudy."

3. The text says, "Her favorite part about secrets was sharing them!"
4. *Spills the beans* means "tells a secret."
5. The author wrote, "Six-year-old Trudy loved secrets. Her favorite part about secrets was sharing them!" *Spills the beans* means to tell a secret, so this is great title.

Knock Knack Noah (Card 53)

1. A sentence that describes a character trait of Noah's is: "Noah was great at being clumsy."
2. A sentence that tells you what Noah had a knack for is: "You could say he had a knack for knocking things over."
3. This sentence tells what happened when Noah bumped the bikes: "They tipped over, one by one, like a line of dominoes."
4. *Knack* means "talent."
5. Noah is great at bowling. The text states: "He rolled the ball, and it knocked down all the pins. Strike!"

Identical . . . Not! (Card 54)

1. A sentence that shows how the sisters are similar is: "They were the same height and had the same haircut." (Other answers possible.)
2. A sentence that shows how the sisters are different is: "In contrast, Alice's passion was sports: soccer, basketball, and long bike rides." (Other answers possible.)
3. According to the story, "They both LOVED going to the movies and sitting side by side."
4. *Strenuous* means "hard and tiring."
5. The text says, "Mia loved books, puzzles, and games. She was a chess fanatic!" I love all those things, too, so I am more like Mia. (Other answers possible.)

Felix Goes Fishing (Card 55)

1. A sentence that states the main theme of the story is: "Honesty is the best policy."
2. Here's a sentence that shows how Felix was rewarded for telling the truth: "The man gave Felix lots of pointers." (Other answers possible.)
3. This sentence tells how long the fishing trip lasted: "He and his family were off on a three-hour fishing expedition!"
4. *Expedition* means "a group trip."
5. Honesty is the best policy because Felix learned how to fish. The author states, "Felix's brothers didn't catch any fish. Felix, however, caught three humongous sea bass."

Spooked (Card 56)

1. A sentence that tells where this story is set is: "Sherman walked down Walnut Street in his Batman costume."
2. The story takes place on Halloween. A sentence that shows this is, "'Trick or treat!' he said, and received two pieces of candy." (Other answers possible.)
3. According to the story, "When he turned, he was looking into the face of a zombie."
4. *Sinister* means "mean."
5. No. The story says, "Sherman screamed, dropping his bag of candy." He would not have been scared if he knew it was Jamal.

That's NOT How You Do It! (Card 57)

1. A sentence that describes Stella's personality is: "Avery's bossy cousin Stella came for a visit." (Other answers possible.)
2. A sentence that describes Stella's appearance is: "Cranky Stella was always glowering."
3. According to the story, "Avery drew a ship on a stormy sea."
4. *Glowering* means "frowning."
5. The text says, "But then Stella shot and missed." That made Avery smile because it proved that Stella did not know everything.

Freshly Fallen Snowman (Card 58)

1. A sentence that states the theme of the story is: "You should leave well enough alone."
2. This sentence describes the new snowman Simone built: "It was just right."
3. The text states, "It was late December."
4. *Furnished* means "provided."
5. This is a great title because the snowman really falls down. The text states, "The heavy gloves caused the sticks to break off, and the whole snowman came tumbling down."

Lemonade for Ice Cream (Card 59)

1. A sentence that shows the conflict is: "Jackie and her brother Jason wanted to buy ice cream cones, but they didn't have any money."
2. The sentence that shows the resolution is: "They earned enough money by selling lemonade to buy two ice cream cones."
3. The story says, "Jackie had an idea."
4. *In no time flat* means "very quickly."
5. No. According to the story, "They made two big pitchers and sold it out on the sidewalk."

Thoughtful Theo (Card 60)

1. This sentence shows that Theo doesn't want his sandwich: "Theo took tiny bites and made a face."
2. This sentence shows that Theo will get his ice cream: "Then Theo's mom reached for her wallet."
3. When Theo set down his sandwich, here's what happened: "Soon pigeons began to peck at it."
4. *Feigning* means "pretending."
5. No. The author wrote: "Theo sat on the park bench with his mom."

Quentin's Rough Start (Card 61)

1. A sentence that shows what Quentin thought about his morning is, "*This is the worst morning ever*, he thought." (Other answers possible.)
2. A sentence that shows things aren't going well for Quentin is, "When he went into the kitchen, there was no more of his favorite cereal." (Other answers possible.)
3. A sentence that contains an onomatopoeia is, "*Beep, beep, beep* went the annoying alarm clock."
4. *Disastrous* means "really bad."
5. The story ends happily. The last sentence says, "Suddenly his day was looking much better!"

Ruby and Ro (Card 62)

1. A sentence that shows similarity in the story is: "Both played on the Lions." (Other answers possible.)
2. A sentence that shows difference in the story is: "While Ruby was a smooth and adept passer, Ro was a super shot."
3. According to the story, "The Lions won!"
4. *Adept* means "skilled."
5. Yes. The text says, "But Ro knew how much credit Ruby deserved."

Felipe vs. the Broccoli Spear (Card 63)

1. A sentence that shows the main conflict is, "Felipe detested green vegetables."
2. A sentence that shows the resolution is, "So he sprinkled a bit of hot sauce on his broccoli spear, and it was pretty tasty!"
3. According to the story, "He loved it on eggs, on pizza, even on popcorn."
4. *Detested* means "hated."
5. No, Felipe likes kale less than broccoli. The text says, "Tonight it was broccoli, but some nights it was spinach or, even worse, kale!"

"That's fine." (Card 64)

1. This sentence shows how Lisa feels when she's picked last: "Lisa looked away and quickly blinked back some tears."
2. This sentence shows how Lisa feels when Renata says she'll pick her first: "This time she broke into a big, happy grin."
3. This sentence tells you what game the kids were playing: "At recess, the kids were choosing teams to play capture the flag."
4. *Distressed* means "unhappy."
5. Renata cares. The story says: "Renata, one of the other kids, was distressed to see Lisa so upset."

Akimi's Brother (Card 65)

1. A sentence that shows what Akimi's brother is like is: "On Halloween, when Akimi was too sick to go trick-or-treating, he shared all his candy with her." (Other answers possible.)
2. A sentence that tells how Akimi feels about her brother is: "Akimi felt so lucky to have such an awesome brother."
3. A sentence that shows how Akimi's brother isn't perfect is: "Sometimes he rolled his eyes at her jokes." (Other answers possible.)
4. *Dreadful* means "terrible."
5. No. The text says, "Sometimes he rolled his eyes at her jokes."

Big Mess Challenge (Card 66)

1. A sentence that shows how Malik and Leo are similar is: "Both were equally good at slithering." (Other answers possible.)
2. A sentence that shows how they are different is: "Leo swang better than Malik." (Other answers possible.)
3. According to the text, "Leo had mud, ketchup, and crushed-up cheese curls all over himself."
4. *Victor* means "winner."
5. The Big Mess Challenge includes ketchup. The story says, "Next, they had to swing on a rope through a ketchup waterfall."

A Movie Muddle (Card 67)

1. A sentence that shows this story's conflict is: "Diya couldn't decide which friend to take to the movies."
2. A sentence that shows the resolution is: "By using the gift card and the money, Diya could take both friends."
3. According to the text, "Her grandma had sent twenty dollars for her birthday."

4. *Cross* means "angry."
5. Yes. The text says, "And they'd even have a few dollars left over for popcorn!"

Marta's Missing Tooth (Card 68)

1. According to the story, "There was a hole in her pocket."
2. According to the story, "The tooth was lost!"
3. A sentence that contains a hyperbole is: "Her smile was a mile wide."
4. *Revealing* means "showing."
5. Marta is proud. The author wrote, "When she saw her grandmother, she smiled proudly, revealing the gap in her smile."

Strange Sounds (Card 69)

1. A sentence that shows this spooky tone is: "Milo lay awake, his eyes wide as saucers." (Other answers possible.)
2. A sentence that shows this relieved tone is: "Milo felt better." (Other answers possible.)
3. When Milo got really scared, this is how he woke up his friend: "He poked his sleeping friend on the shoulder."
4. *Soothing* means "calming."
5. No. The text states: "He drifted off to sleep."

Unplugged Saturday (Card 70)

1. One sentence that shows Lexi is unhappy about Unplugged Saturday is, "She thought this was going to be the most boring day of her entire life." (Other answers possible.)
2. A sentence that shows that Lexi changes her mind is, "She never would have had this much fun with her brother if it hadn't been for Unplugged Saturday!" (Other answers possible.)
3. According to the story, "Unplugged Saturday meant no TV, no video games, and no computer for the whole day."
4. *Sulked* means "felt sad."
5. Yes. According to the story: "Lexi had a blast!"

Learning the Rules (Card 71)

1. A sentence that describes a character trait of Grady's personality is: "Grady was very greedy."
2. A sentence that tells you the name of the board game is: "It was called Zilcho."
3. The story says, "Grady had never played it before."
4. *Object* means "goal."

5. The end of the story says: "So Grady learned the game's rules. He also learned to be less greedy."

Ears, the Rabbit (Card 72)
1. A sentence that shows where the story takes place is: "She and her dad arrived at the pet store just as it was opening."
2. A sentence that shows what day the story takes place is: "It was April 17th—also known as Min's birthday."
3. A sentence with a simile is: "He was as cute as a button!"
4. *Droopy* means "hanging."
5. Min chose the name Ears because, "The bunny was brown with long droopy ears."

Paint Problems (Card 73)
1. A sentence that states the theme of the story is: "Learn from your mistakes."
2. Lin did this to keep from making the mistake a third time: "She finished her lunch on the stairs to make sure she didn't sit in paint again."
3. According to the story, here's how the chair looked in the end: "Once the paint dried, the chair looked awesome."
4. *Realization* means "understanding."
5. No. The story says, "She chose bright orange for hers."

Otto Makes a Break for It (Card 74)
1. This sentence tells where the story takes place: "Otto the Octopus had been living for three years at the aquarium."
2. A sentence that shows when this story takes place is: "At night, when the aquarium workers had gone home, he nudged the top off his tank."
3. The story states, "He didn't mind living in his glass tank, but he missed the ocean, where he used to live." (Other answers possible.)
4. *Make a break for it* means "run away."
5. Otto considers the sea home. The story says, "Just as he'd hoped, the pipe led him back to the sea. He was home at last!"

On Your Mark, Get Set . . . Stop! (Card 75)
1. A sentence that states the cause is: "All Malika had to hear was the command to start a race: *On your mark, get set, go!*"
2. A sentence that states the effect is: "Then she'd run as fast as her two legs could carry her."

3. This is what happened when Malika realized what had actually been said: "She stopped running and started laughing."
4. *Strides* means "long steps."
5. The text says, "Malika was the fastest runner on the track team."

The Star (Card 76)
1. A sentence that shows that the tone of this story is boastful is, "My acting skills are stellar, and I just have a natural star quality." (Other answers possible.)
2. A sentence that shows how Clive's classmates view him is: "Some kids think I'm stuck on myself."
3. Clive says, "Actually, I'm playing a tree."
4. *Slighted* means "insulted."
5. No. The story says: "I don't even have any lines."

The Cat in the House (Card 77)
1. A sentence that shows the grumpy tone is, "I don't know how humans can stand such a pest." (Other answers possible.)
2. A sentence that shows the humans think the *dog* is the annoying one is, "Whenever I chase him, they say 'Poor kitty' and 'Bad dog!'"
3. A sentence containing two onomatopoeias is: "No, he meows and purrs!"
4. *Pathetic* means "ridiculous."
5. No. The first sentence says, "I'm a dog."

Nixing a Nickname (Card 78)
1. A sentence that shows this story's conflict is: "Gary did not like the nickname Kelvyn had given him: 'Goofball Gary.'"
2. A sentence that shows the resolution is: "He talked calmly to Kelvyn to make him think about hurtful nicknames."
3. According to the text, this is why Gary decided not to give Kelvyn a hurtful nickname: "Two wrongs didn't make a right."
4. *Contemplated* means "thought about."
5. The boys become friends. The text says, "Soon, Gary and Kelvyn even became friends."

Samson Runs Off (Card 79)
1. A sentence that shows where the first part of the story is set is: "They settled on a blanket in the park."
2. According to the text, "There on the front porch was Samson, waiting for them to return."

3. According to the text, "Kwamie was heartbroken."
4. *Trudged* means "walked slowly."
5. No. The story states, "When the fireworks began thundering overhead, Samson got spooked and took off."

Rained Out (Card 80)
1. A sentence that shows the story's conflict is: "His big day was going to be ruined!"
2. A sentence that shows the story's resolution is: "So they all put on their raincoats and headed out to the theater."
3. According to the story, "When he woke up on Saturday, he noticed that the sky was very dark."
4. *Alternate* means "another."
5. Yes. The text states, "Sam had a great time."

Finders Keepers? (Card 81)
1. A sentence that shows Manuel is a kind person is: "So he ran after the man and gave him back the twenty dollars." (Other answers possible.)
2. A sentence that shows that the man feels grateful is: "He had a giant ice cream cone for Manuel, along with plenty of thanks."
3. The author says, "Manuel jumped up and grabbed it."
4. *Unaware* means "not knowing."
5. No. The story says, "Manuel thought how bad he would feel if he lost all that money. So he ran after the man and gave him back the twenty dollars." (Other answers possible.)

Moat Party (Card 82)
1. A sentence that tells where this story takes place is, "She lived in a big, stone castle in a land called Calazee."
2. A sentence that tells when this story takes place is, "It was long, long ago in the Middle Ages."
3. According to the text, these were Ann's duties: "She had to attend ceremonies and do lots of bowing and waving."
4. *Annual* means "yearly."
5. Yes, her party was a success. The text says, "It was the hit of the kingdom!" (Other answers possible.)

The Perfect Pet (Card 83)
1. A sentence that shows the conflict in this story is: "They could not decide what kind of dog to get." (Other answers possible.)

2. A sentence that shows how this conflict is resolved is: "So they got a golden doodle, and they were both thrilled."
3. According to the story, "Their mom explained that a golden doodle was a cross between a golden retriever and a poodle."
4. *Compromise* means "deal."
5. It has a happy ending. The last sentence says, "So they got a golden doodle, and they were both thrilled."

Ruler of the Universe (Card 84)
1. This sentence tells you that the alien is make-believe: "Dave had done a very fine job of acting." (Other answers possible.)
2. This sentence tells you that Dave is different from the cruel space alien that he plays: "Dave answered his phone in a friendly voice." (Other answers possible.)
3. Here's the first thing Dave did after he was done filming for the day: "He walked over and got an apple juice."
4. *Amiably* means "in a friendly way."
5. Dave is a good actor. The story states, "Dave had done a very fine job of acting." (Other answers possible.)

My Friend Inez (Card 85)
1. A sentence that describes Inez's personality is, "She was kind and never said mean things about people." (Other answers possible.)
2. According to the story, "Sometimes popular kids thought they were superior to everyone else, but Inez was nice to everyone."
3. The author says, "They felt bad about their mean behavior and stopped picking on others." (Other answers possible.)
4. *Superior* means "better."
5. Yes, she would be a great friend. The text says, "She was kind and never said mean things about people." (Other answers possible.)

Hangry Jack (Card 86)
1. A sentence that shows this angry tone is: "Riding in the car had grown irritating." (Other answers possible.)
2. Another sentence that shows this angry tone is: "Even seeing mountains and deer wasn't fun anymore." (Other answers possible.)
3. According to the story: "*Hungry* plus *angry* = *hangry*."
4. *Grimace* means "a very unhappy look."

5. The text says, "Suddenly, the whole world just seemed so much better and Jack felt awesome."

Two Weeks at Camp (Card 87)
1. A sentence that describes Mitchell's personality is, "He was quiet and shy."
2. A sentence that describes Mitchell's cabinmates is, "They were friendly and outgoing."
3. This sentence tells where the story is set: "The camp was in the Ozark Mountains, 150 miles from home."
4. *Dreading* means "fearing."
5. The first sentence says, "When Mitchell arrived at summer camp, his stomach was tied in knots." That means he felt scared.

Gabby, the Goalie (Card 88)
1. A sentence that shows this nervous tone is: "Little beads of sweat formed on Gabby's forehead." (Other answers possible.)
2. Another sentence that shows this nervous tone is: "Gabby's legs went kind of wobbly." (Other answers possible.)
3. A saying that compares nervousness to an insect is: "She had butterflies in her stomach."
4. *Composed* means "calm."
5. Yes. The author writes: "Just like that, Gabby became composed and confident."

Flying High (Card 89)
1. A sentence that shows this is, "Martine opened her eyes and saw her mom's face, and the light blue walls of her room."
2. At the end of the story, a sentence that shows when the story takes place is: "It was Monday morning, time to get up and go to school."
3. A sentence that shows what Martine sees while she's flying is, "Martine flew over her school and saw her friends out at recess." (Other answers possible.)
4. *Uttering* means "saying."
5. She likes flying. The text says, "It was the best feeling ever." (Other answers possible.)

Which Watch? (Card 90)
1. The story says, "Both had faces that lit up in the dark." (Other answers possible)
2. The story says, "The digital watch displayed the time in numbers, but the analog watch used hands to show the time." (Other answers possible.)

3. According to the story, "Dexter ended up choosing the analog watch because it had a cool camouflage band."
4. *Displayed* means "showed."
5. No. The author wrote, "His grandmother took him shopping so he could pick out the perfect one."

Slurp! Smack! (Card 91)
1. A sentence that states the cause is: "Someone would place a bowl of spaghetti in front of Bart."
2. A sentence that states the effect is: "Bart would slurp up the noodles, one by one."
3. According to the story, "Bart loved spaghetti more than anything!"
4. *Chagrin* means "nervous embarrassment."
5. Yes. The last sentence says, "The meal tasted grand and was super silly—just the way Bart liked it." (Other answers possible.)

Hey, That Dog Looks Just Like Me! (Card 92)
1. A sentence that shows Charlie is young is: "Charlie was a three-month-old pup that had never seen a mirror before."
2. A sentence that shows how Charlie feels when the other dog doesn't want to play is: "Charlie felt sad that the dog didn't want to play."
3. A sentence in the story that contains a simile is: "Charlie and the dog were like two peas in a pod."
4. *Gazing* means "looking."
5. Charlie likes playing with the girl who lived in the house. The last sentence says, "She was much *more* fun than that silly dog."

Fixing a Fight (Card 93)
1. A sentence that shows this story's conflict is: "Now Merry was mad and stormed off in a huff."
2. A sentence that shows the resolution is: "She decided to send Merry a special text to show her how much she cared."
3. According to the story, "She'd been so busy with homework that she hadn't even looked at her phone."
4. *Remedy* means "fix."
5. The story says, "BBFFAA = Best-Best Friends Forever And Always."

Kamal's Choice (Card 94)

1. A sentence that shows the theme of the story is: "Now Kamal understood that he had to choose to work if he wanted to be good at something."
2. A sentence that shows Kamal's new attitude is: "He practiced every day over the next six months."
3. According to the text, "'At the next recital, Kamal got a standing ovation!"
4. *Majestic* means "grand."
5. This is a great title because Kamal had to make a hard choice. The text states, "Now Kamal understood that he had to choose to work if he wanted to be good at something." (Other answers possible.)

Bedtime for Fireflies (Card 95)

1. A sentence that tells where this story takes place is, "The fireflies hung out on the cool, shady underside of a leaf."
2. A sentence that tells when this story takes place is, "It was 7:00 A.M., and the sun shone brightly."
3. According to the story, instead of going to sleep, the firefly kids did this: "They kept fluttering their wings and lighting up their tails."
4. *Snug* means "cozy and comfortable."
5. No. The author wrote, "But the firefly kids were too excited to sleep." (Other answers possible.)

Couch Calm (Card 96)

1. A sentence that shows this peaceful tone is: "Deon took off his shoes, stretched out on the couch, and relaxed." (Other answers possible.)
2. Another sentence that shows the peaceful tone is: "It was so calm with nobody fighting over the remote." (Other answers possible.)
3. According to the text, this was Deon's snack: "Deon made a big bowl of popcorn."
4. *Bliss* means "peaceful joy."
5. No. The last sentence says, "*Oh well*, thought Deon, *it was nice while it lasted.*"

The Prankster (Card 97)

1. A sentence that describes Gus's personality is: "Gus was a mischievous guy." (Other answers possible.)
2. Another sentence that describes his personality is: "He always played pranks on people." (Other answers possible.)
3. This sentence tells about the prank Gus played on his brother: "He put a pickle in his little brother's shoe."
4. *Contents* means "what's contained in something."
5. The text says, "Gus had pranked himself!" (Other answers possible.)

A Leaf's Life (Card 98)

1. A sentence that shows where the story is set is: "She had been the brightest on her tree branch."
2. A sentence that shows what season the story takes place in is: "But now it was October, and she was a dull, crispy brown."
3. According to the story, "As the weather changed, Annette turned a lovely, bright red."
4. *Hue* means "color."
5. Yes. The text states, "She was quite nervous about falling, but most of her pals had already made the journey." (Other answers possible.)

Enjoying a Cloud Show (Card 99)

1. A sentence that tells where this story takes place is, "Tanya sat on a country hillside."
2. A sentence that tells when this story takes place is, "It was a warm summer afternoon."
3. According to the story, "It was shaped almost exactly like Australia."
4. *Resembled* means "looked like."
5. No. The story says, "Last, it looked like a llama balancing a beach ball on its nose."

The Twin Twins (Card 100)

1. A sentence that shows how Ava and Abby are alike is: "They looked alike, with blue eyes and blond hair." (Other answers possible.)
2. A sentence that shows how the twins are different is: "Ava played the guitar, while Abby played the drums." (Other answers possible.)
3. This sentence tells what instruments the other band members played: "They met another set of twins who played the piano and bass."
4. *Combination* means "the mixing of different parts."
5. No. The text states, "And guess what they called their band? The Twin Twins!"